D0350344

THE BOOK OF WHAT IF...?

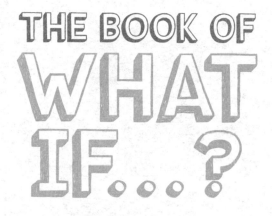

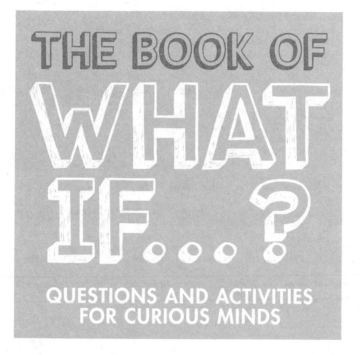

THE BOOK OF
WHAT IF...?

QUESTIONS AND ACTIVITIES
FOR CURIOUS MINDS

Matt Murrie and Andrew R McHugh

ALADDIN
New York London Toronto Sydney New Delhi

BEYOND WORDS
Hillsboro, Oregon

ALADDIN
An imprint of Simon & Schuster
Children's Publishing Division
1230 Avenue of the Americas
New York, NY 10020

BEYOND WORDS
20827 N.W. Cornell Road, Suite 500
Hillsboro, Oregon 97124-9808
503-531-8700 / 503-531-8773 fax
www.beyondword.com

Managing Editor: Lindsay S. Easterbrooks-Brown
Copyeditors: Kristin Thiel, Emmalisa Sparrow
Proofreader: Linda M. Meyer
Interior and cover design: Sara E. Blum
The text of this book was set in Adobe Devanagari and Interstate.

For information about special discounts for bulk purchases, please contact
Simon & Schuster Special Sales at 1-866-506-1949 or business@simonandschuster.com.

The Simon & Schuster Speakers Bureau can bring authors to your live event. For more
information or to book an event contact the Simon & Schuster Speakers Bureau at
1-866-248-3049 or visit our website at www.simonspeakers.com.

Manufactured in the United States of America 0316 RR2

10 9 8 7 6 5 4 3 2 1

Library of Congress Cataloging-in-Publication Data

Names: Murrie, Matthew, author. | McHugh, Andrew R, author.
Title: The book of what if...? : questions and activities for curious minds / by
    Matt Murrie and Andrew R McHugh.
Description: Beyond Words/Aladdin edition. | New York : Aladdin ; Hillsboro,
    Oregon : Beyond Words, 2016. | Audience: Ages 8-12. | Audience:
    Grades 4 to 6. | Includes bibliographical references and index.
Identifiers: LCCN 2015033441| ISBN 9781582705293 (hardcover : alk. paper) |
    ISBN 9781481430746 (ebook)
Subjects: LCSH: Curiosities and wonders—Juvenile literature. | Children's
    questions and answers. | Thought and thinking—Juvenile literature.
Classification: LCC AG243 .M857 2016 | DDC 031—dc23
LC record available at http://lccn.loc.gov/2015033441

Contents

Preface

Do you ever feel like the world is celebrating Opposite Day every day? But what if everybody saw things exactly the way you did? Would we all be better off . . . or worse? Be honest! Have you ever looked at something and thought, "Hmm, what if this one thing could be different?" and then explored what life would be like if it was in fact different? That process typically starts with a question. "What if no one went to bed hungry?" "What if we could go to the moon?" "What if we wrote a book about questions?" The best part is that anyone can ask a question—not only "experts" but those just beginning their journeys to become experts.

We're not experts on any of the topics in this book—but we are insanely curious. We wrote this book together anyways because we believe in the power of, "What if . . . ?" We believe in it so much that we started a company in 2010 dedicated to turning ideas into action. You see, we view curiosity as a natural resource. The same way people (including us) are concerned about wasting natural resources such as oil, coal, and natural gas, we're especially concerned about curiosity.

How can we stop wasting curiosity?

For some people, it's letting them know it's OK to be curious. For others, it's helping them find ways to take action on what they're curious about. Some just need to realize that being curious is a powerful ability to have. Through conferences, workshops, content, and connecting people, we've spread curiosity all around the world. Now you're a part of this movement to make the world a more curious place. Thank you!

Why ask, "What if?" Because nobody knows what tomorrow holds, and yesterday's lessons are never complete. By asking, you're taking the first step toward doing. Every great, world-shaking action starts with an idea. That idea becomes a seed that can then grow and spread beyond the mind that planted it. But nothing grows, spreads, or happens without being planted first. What if it's up to you to first think and then do? What if you do and then think? What if combining these two actions can create more awesome for you and beyond you? It's amazing all the things that become possible later on when you start with two simple words: *what if.*

As you read this book, you might find new answers to old questions. You might find old answers to new questions. You might not find any answers at all. That's OK! This isn't a textbook. There won't be a test when you're done reading it. Instead, we hope that by reading this book, you develop new insights, perspectives, and curiosities about yourself and the world we all share. Don't forget to occasionally put this book down while reading to start doing amazing stuff.

As we explore our questions, we also ask questions of you, the reader. This is part of the beauty of questions: They beg for participation. Each question starts an exploration of even more questions. Some entries go even further with expert interviews and historical spotlights, so we can learn directly from interesting people doing amazing things. There is peer introspection—we've posed these very same questions to kids just like you. We also have illustrations to illuminate complex ideas, and there are even technical corners, where you can learn more about how and why something is the way it is. Our most frequent element other than questions is activities that help you actively think about the questions. So get ready.

You can read alone or read as a group in class. You can talk with your friends about the book. Participate in activities. Ask your own questions. The only wrong way to use this book is to finish reading it with the same level of curiosity and the same beliefs you started with. Some of these questions deal with topics that are only going to grow more important in our world, like genetic modification, artificial intelligence (AI), and life extension. It's important for us to deal with these topics earlier rather than later—to have the time to understand them and maybe even improve upon them before these technologies become ever present in our lives. This way, by asking, "What if . . . ?," we can guide where we go in the future instead of waiting until the future is here and all we can ask is, "Now what?"

The Book of What If . . . ? is designed to spark your curiosity on certain ideas and open windows into worlds you may not have realized exist. That was our job in writing this book. Your job now is to go beyond (far beyond!) reading it. We expect you to interact with the information between these covers. There are other people out there wanting to collaborate with you to start something awesome. So, what are you waiting for? The world is waiting for you!

Your fellow wonderers,

Matt Murrie and Andrew R McHugh

Part 1
History

History: a long time ago. Right?

Kind of. History is everything that has happened before right now. It has stories of kings and queens, tribes turning into empires, technological improvements that changed the course of a country's development, and the occasional toppling of a dynasty.

What if history is also advice for the future? Some people say that history repeats itself. Well, not quite. Humans definitely make similar mistakes, but there are always new warning signals to teach us better ways to do things. What if, by looking back at these mistakes, we can make sure we don't make them, exactly, again?

What if we can also examine where we are now by thinking of alternative histories? For instance, what if we had never landed on the moon? Or what if dinosaurs still existed? These questions help us think about how we got here and how to get to where we want to be.

Another thing to think about is, if you're moving through a scale of time with the past behind you and the future ahead of you, this very moment, you're making your own history.

What if you're writing the history book of your life right now?

What if Dinosaurs Hadn't Gone Extinct?

If you've done any digging around on dinosaurs, you've probably discovered that the word *dinosaur* means "terrible lizard."[1] But this isn't entirely true. The actual translation for the Greek prefix *deinos* is "fearfully great." The inventor of the word *dinosaur*, Richard Owen, intended the word to inspire awe, not terror.[2] Over time, people have turned "fearfully great" into simply "terrible."

The second half of the word *dinosaur* comes from the Greek word *sauros*, which means "lizard."[3] Even though many originally thought dinosaurs were lizards, scientists have now determined that they weren't. Interestingly enough, birds and lizards both seem to be descendants of dinosaurs (though different ones).[4] The more we learn about dinosaurs, the more ways we find how they differed from the reptiles we have today, including lizards.

But what if we had more than just a bunch of bones to go by to understand dinosaurs? What if dinosaurs were alive today?

There are several questions to consider here. Perhaps the most urgent one is: who would "rule" the earth—dinosaurs or humans?

Looking around today, humans have been able to create an existence at the top of the food chain, and we've been able to develop

> "I would have a pet velociraptor. And we could buy dinosaurs at dino dealerships because there would be no need for cars because you just ride your T. Rex where you need to go."
> —Charlie, Battle High School, age 15

> "I would train a dinosaur to let me ride it to school."
> —Andrew, Battle High School, age 15

technologies that move us further from the natural world. Do you think humans could have evolved in this manner if we had to compete against (or run away from!) dinosaurs all day long?

> "The bigger dinosaurs would be hunted and the smaller ones domesticated as animals of labor."
> —Jonathan, Battle High School, age 17

What if, instead of finding a neighbor's dog digging a hole in your yard, you saw a triceratops digging a hole? What if, instead of being afraid of bee stings when playing outside, you had to look out for pterodactyls swooping down from the sky to scoop you up for dinner? What if every day on your way to school, you were chased by a *Tyrannosaurus rex*? Could you tell your teacher a *T. rex* ate your homework?

Where would we be today? What would be better? What would be worse?

ACTIVITY
Dino-Proof Your House

Imagine you live in a neighborhood struggling with an overpopulation of dinosaurs. They're everywhere! Many people have come home to find dinosaurs in their yards eating their plants and leaves off their trees. Some homes have even been stepped on by dinosaurs—and crushed to smithereens, of course. What do you do? How can you save your home?

Draw a picture of what your home would look like once it's been "dino-proofed."

MARY ANNING, DINO-DISCOVERER

If you look around, you'll notice that there are not many creatures that look like the ones that were alive in the time of dinosaurs. The dinosaurs went extinct and some of them were fossilized. Many, many years later, a set of apes evolved into humans, and many years after that, we started fossil hunting. Mary Anning was an expert fossil hunter.

Sometime between 1809 and 1811, when she was only 10 to 12 years old, Anning and her brother found one of the first ichthyosaur fossils (an ichthyosaur looks kind of like a dolphin). Her whole family hunted fossils, but Anning was the most dedicated. She went on to find many other ichthyosaur fossils, but her greatest find was of the first plesiosaur (a swimming dinosaur with a long neck like a giraffe).

"If dinosaurs never went extinct, humans would have very slim chances of survival with how dangerous the world around us would be. Perhaps this would create a different society that focuses more on survival and protection rather than the society we have developed in which survival isn't always immediately on our minds."
—Dillon, Battle High School, age 16

Anning was a well versed paleontologist (person who studies fossils), an expert at finding, drawing, and analyzing skeletal remains of dinosaurs.[5]

What if the Mongol Empire Helped the United States' Westward Expansion?

Stretching from the Pacific Ocean to the Danube River, the Mongol Empire still holds the place as the largest, contiguous empire of all time.[6] The Mongol Empire was so massive that during its reign (1270–1309), it contained over 25 percent of the world's population and 16 percent of the planet's land mass.[7] With a reach that large, Mongols had a huge influence on the world—then and on into today.

For example, in an empire as vast as this one, quick communication was critical to keeping things going—and keeping them from falling apart. To make sure everyone was always in the loop, Mongols developed a messenger system called the *yam*.[8] The yam was a system of postal relay stations at which riders carrying

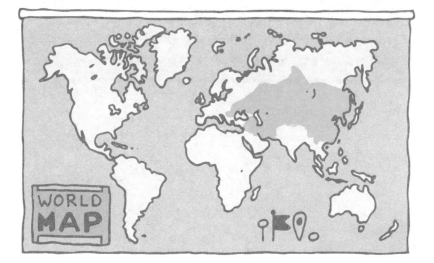

messages on horseback could rest, refuel, or exchange their tired horse for a fresh one. Sound familiar? A few hundred years later, the United States would replicate this same system as the Pony Express to facilitate its communication during westward expansion.[9]

GENGHIS KHAN, CONQUEROR OF CONQUERORS

As ginormous as the Mongol Empire was, it can be traced back to the vision and ambition of a single person: Genghis Khan. In the wake of his time on earth, history remembers Genghis Khan as both a great destroyer and a great creator.

Historians calculate Genghis Khan was directly responsible for the deaths of nearly 40 million people. Census data from the Middle Ages during Genghis Khan's reign show China's total population dropping by tens of millions. Genghis Khan's attacks were so devastating, historians estimate his war with the Khwarezmid Empire (located in what is Iran today), killed three-fourths of that entire population. In all, it's believed the great Genghis Khan lowered the population of the entire world while he was living in it by 11 percent.[10]

However, it turns out Genghis Khan was a lover as well as a fighter. Geneticists believe that approximately 16 million people on the planet today are direct descendants of Genghis Khan.[11]

What if Europeans Had Never Landed in the Americas?

One big difference would be the name. The name America comes from Italian explorer and cartographer (someone who makes maps) Amerigo Vespucci. But it wasn't Vespucci's ego that put his name on the map. It was another cartographer, Martin Waldscemüller.[12]

Shortly after Columbus, Vespucci crossed the Atlantic to explore what the Europeans saw as the New World and mapped out much of what is now South America. Waldseemüller used Vespucci's maps to draw the world map he created in 1507.

Waldseemüller wasn't necessarily trying to name the continent of what is now South America after Vespucci; he was only giving him credit for the information he used in his new world map. However, his map (one of the first to include the continents of the New World[13]) became so popular that people began referring to the New World as the Americas before anyone could actually name it. The rest, as they say, is history.

> "The country would probably be named something else. Indigenous people would still be here. They would probably not be advanced a lot."
> —Aidan, Columbia Elementary, age 10

> "If the Europeans never landed in the Americas I think that Asians would had landed next, but the indigenous people might have a couple decades more to live in peace."
> —Talia, Columbia Elementary, age 11

Another difference we might notice today is our form of democracy. People often credit the ancient Greeks for the basis of the democracy that took root in the United States of America. However, democracy today is quite different from what the Greeks practiced. What if there is a different group of people responsible for today's democracy? And what if they were living in America long before the Europeans settled it?

Since the United States had just fought a revolution against England, and most people in the American colonies had left Europe to pursue a better life, the colonists weren't very keen on looking to the kingdoms of Europe to construct their new set of laws.

"Where would we be if Europeans never landed in America? Would we live in a town call Koopazoo in some land far away? Would we speak any language we know of? Would we even be alive?"

—Hilary, Columbia Elementary, age 11

Even if their actions didn't always reflect it, many European Americans held great respect (perhaps even envy) for the indigenous peoples' way of life.[14] The admiration the US Founding Fathers had for the Iroquois, in particular, was so great that they modeled the first copy of the US Constitution after the Iroquois Great Law of Peace.[15]

ACTIVITY
Name a New Land

What if you hear on the news that a new island was recently discovered in the middle of the ocean, and there's a contest to name it. Write your answers to these questions on a piece of paper to enter your name into the contest.

1. Proposed name:
2. Who or what does this name come from?
3. Why are you proposing this name?
4. Are there other people, places, or things that share a similar name?
5. Does your name have any symbolic or hidden meaning?

"The country would probably be named something else. Indigenous people would still be here. They would probably not be advanced a lot."
—Aidan, Columbia Elementary, age 10

"The Europeans discovered the Americas in 1492, but one of the first countries to discover the Americas was actually China, so you might speak Chinese."
—Zephyr, Columbia Elementary, age 11

"I think that the indigenous peoples might still have all their land and, don't take this the wrong way, but we would not be here."
—Lyn Marie, Columbia Elementary, age 10

"If the Europeans never landed in the Americas, people would still think the world was flat. The indigenous people would still live here."
—Isaac, Columbia Elementary, age 11

"Then maybe people from Africa or Asia would land in the Americas, and everyone would be a different race at first, but then the Europeans would eventually migrate here."
—Jeremy, Findley Elementary, age 10

What if Humans Had Never Landed on the Moon?

For most of human existence, we've been stuck on a big rock speeding through space called Earth. We've been here looking out at the sky. Most nights, we can see another rock, the moon, which orbits our rock.

What do you think is the most important thing humanity got out of landing on the moon? Some say Tang, Velcro, and pens that write upside down are the most important things to come out of the space program. However, Tang[16] and Velcro[17] were invented before NASA's mission to the moon. Going to the moon just made them famous. Yet the Apollo program did produce technologies you probably find useful today. You know that spring you feel in your step when you're wearing your sneakers? Many sneaker insoles are made out of the same material that was first used in the space boots that made that giant leap on the moon.[18] And your parents may hate cleaning, but at least they can do it with lightweight, cordless devices. You can thank the Apollo program for helping develop lightweight, cordless tools.[19] Imagine how long the extension cord would have been had the astronauts needed one to plug in the tools they used on the moon!

Even with the marvelous technologies that came out of the Apollo program, many think the most important thing that came from landing on the moon was the power to create the dreams of tomorrow. Going to the moon propelled us. Space exploration encourages us to push human potential and excites students to become astronauts, scientists, and explorers. Space travel is the beginning of our species colonizing different planets. Can anyone say "living options?" If we are limited to only one planet (like we are now), all of humanity could get wiped out by a large disaster. What if it's kind of dangerous to be a single-planet civilization?

What if an asteroid hit us? What if a deadly virus started infecting everyone? Or what if zombies happened?! Humans would be trapped in one place, Earth. But if we look to our success with visiting the moon as our first step toward living on other planets, our species might know a less risky existence. If there were a disaster on one rock, at least the humans on the other rock would be safe.

Unfortunately, though, our exploration of space has started to slow. Did you know that after we first landed on the moon, July 20, 1969, scientists believed it would take only another ten years for a human to land on Mars?[20] In the time since then, we've landed a couple of robots on Mars but haven't managed to send any humans. In fact, the last time a human set foot on any space-rock was the moon in 1972. Over forty years ago!

Stepping foot on the moon is something only a few humans have ever experienced. But there are many things we all benefit from that came out of getting those feet up there. Why do you think we've never gone back? Why do you think we slowed down our space exploration? What do you think you can do to make sure humans never stop exploring?

NEIL DeGRASSE TYSON, ASTROPHYSICIST

The day you stop [cosmic exploration], I fear for the future of the species because it's that which distinguishes humans from all other animals. That we explore and understand what we're doing while we're at it and expand our place in the cosmos. And, if that stops, I don't want to live in those times.[21]

Neil deGrasse Tyson is a world-renowned astrophysicist known for his many public appearances and playful demeanor. He's afraid that if we don't put our money into space exploration, we'll diminish ourselves as a species. Tyson has written many books, hosted numerous television shows, and served on both presidential and NASA advisory committees. He is the fifth head of the Hayden Planetarium in New York City.[22] In a lot of his work, he attempts to make space science interesting and exciting. If he can do that, then maybe the next generation of kids growing up will decide to focus some of their energy on going to space. Maybe the next great space adventurer or scientist is you.

ACTIVITY
Where Next? Meet Up

Gather yourself and at least three friends to a chat. The topic? Decide where humanity should adventure to if we could only explore one more place. What or where does your group think humans should focus on exploring next? Why? It's OK if deciding means arguing to agreement.

TECHNICAL CORNER
Rockets and Rocket Ships

Rocket ships and the people who fly them are pretty amazing. We take huge chunks of metal, strap people to them, start a controlled explosion behind them, and launch them into space. We must be bonkers.

Rocket development started way back around 400 BC, when Greeks were playing with steam. Throughout the years, Chinese scientists created arrows with rocket tips—Mongols started building them too—and Germans developed multistage rockets (rockets within rockets). It wasn't until 1898 that a Russian schoolteacher, Konstantin Tsiolkovsky, started thinking that rockets could take us to space.[23]

Sir Isaac Newton formalized three laws of motion. The third law says that for every action, there is an equal and opposite reaction. If you push your friend with three pounds of force, your friend moves away from you with three pounds of force, while at the same time your muscles exert three pounds of force. With rockets, this means that if there is an explosion with one hundred thousand pounds of force, the metal just in front of the explosion will move forward with one hundred thousand pounds of force, minus whatever part of the explosion that doesn't push the rocket up.

If you stand on top of a powerful explosion, you could go to space. (But really, don't do that. It is super dangerous. That's why there are rocket scientists.)

WHAT'S INSIDE A ROCKET?

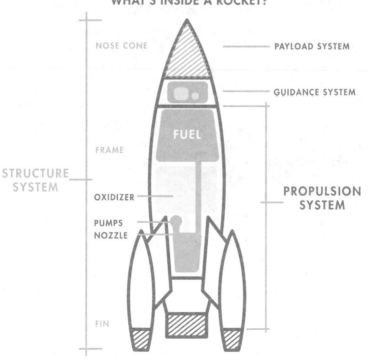

NOSE CONE

PAYLOAD SYSTEM

GUIDANCE SYSTEM

FUEL

FRAME

STRUCTURE SYSTEM

OXIDIZER

PROPULSION SYSTEM

PUMPS
NOZZLE

FIN

What if You Could Travel in Time?

Scientists, writers, and dreamers have always been fascinated by time travel. As we experience our universe, there are three spacial dimensions (which we travel when walking forward and backward, left and right, and up and down) and one temporal (which we travel by moving through time). When you meet up with someone, what do you tell them? You tell them, "Let's meet at 123 Main Street"—which describes a point in two dimensions—"on the third floor"—the location in the third spacial dimension—"at 3:30 PM"—the location in time.

Since you can move forward and backward, left and right, up and down, you can move in any direction in the three spacial dimensions. You can only go forward in time, the temporal dimension.

But what if you could also go backward?

Imagine that one day as you're out walking, you come to a small field. In the middle of the field, there's a chair with seat belts on it and a clock in front of it. You sit down and realize: *this is a time machine.* What would you do next?

Would you travel in time? Which way would you go first? Would you want to go to the first or last moments of the universe? Would

> "I would go back in time to observe history and refine the history book based on what truly happened, not just the opinion of one side of humankind."
> —Charlie, Battle High School, age 15

you want to meet your great-great-great-great-great-great grand-parents or meet your great-great-great-great-great-great grandkids?

Would you use the machine for good or evil? You could go to the past and bring knowledge of vaccines to doctors before the bubonic plague and Spanish flu started, saving millions and millions of lives. Or you could take the personal gain approach: travel to the future to grab the answers to a test

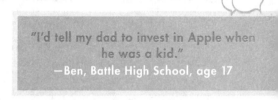

"I'd tell my dad to invest in Apple when he was a kid."
—Ben, Battle High School, age 17

you'll be taking in class next week. You could even go back in time and put money in a bank. Then go forward in time to when your money has grown. Instant riches!

What if everyone could travel in time? How do you think society would change? It would be hard to test people if they could always go and find the answers. What about when people die? Would it still be sad? Someone would never really be dead—that person would exist in a certain segment of time you could always go back and visit.

ACTIVITY
Go Back

Write a short story about traveling back in time. Where would you go? What would you do there? Who would you meet? Would you bring anyone back to the present with you?

ACTIVITY
Go Forward

Now that you've gone backward, let's go forward! Again, write about where you would go and what you would do there. Who would you meet? What would you do there? Would you bring anyone back to the present with you?

ACTIVITY
Create a Time-Lapse

A time-lapse is a video that was taken over a long period of time and then shortened. For example, if you've ever seen a video of a seed growing into a stalk and then leaves, that's a time-lapse! These videos are kind of like short time machines. Imagine that if you were in a time machine moving forward in time more quickly than usual (and assuming you could see outside of the machine), the world could look like one big time-lapse.

"I would travel to the fortieth century, grab cool gadgets and stuff, and come back and be super cool."
—John Ryan, Battle High School, age 15

Now it's your turn. Shoot a short video and speed it up.

TECHNICAL CORNER
Building a Time Machine

While physicists used to cast time travel as silly, there are a few that are now exploring the topic seriously.[24] Mathematicians and physicists found proof that time travel can work within our current understanding of the world. (Doesn't that make you want to study science?) Many of the devices they've come up with to help us move through time require vast amounts of energy (and a weird negative energy)—way beyond what we're able to build today.[25] A device suggested by theoretical physicist Kip Thorne uses two sets of metal plates, each charged with large amounts of electricity.[26] These plates would create a small tear in space-time. Then you could take one of the sets of plates, put it on a spaceship, and send the spaceship away from Earth at near the speed of light. Since objects traveling at close to the speed of light experience time much more slowly, the first and second sets of plates would work at different points in time. Boom! You've made a time machine.

Now you just have to make sure you can enter it without being hurt![27]

"You would create a paradox that would destroy the universe."
—Conner, Battle High School, age 15

"If I could travel in time, I would go back in time and invent the time machine, but this would cause several problems. If the time machine was invented any sooner, would I still have been the first person to go back in time and invent it?"
—Dillon, Battle High School, age 16

What if There Were
Never Books?

Books. A bunch of words on a bunch of pages, right? Yet there are few things people love and hate as much as books. You might despise a textbook but not be able to take your hands off other books (like this one!). People have even burned books because they viewed them as dangerous. Beyond giving you a few paper cuts or a bruise on the head (if one is thrown at you), how can books be dangerous?

Books don't just contain words. What if it's the ideas in them that make books so powerful—or dangerous?

What if there never were any books written? People could still communicate ideas verbally, but books allow ideas to spread across greater distances of space and time. Think about your favorite book. If there weren't any books, you'd only be able to hear the ideas and stories of the authors while they were alive. Imagine how many great stories would be lost! And now with the internet, writing continues to spread, more ideas can be shared, and authors-long-gone can still have a voice.

There was a time before books and writing. As it turns out, being in a culture or group of people who can read—even if you cannot read—changes how you think. Catch that? Not only can books teach you *about* things to think about, they can also teach you *how* to think about things. Researchers found that if you and

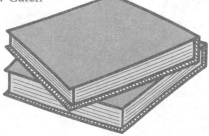

everyone around you never developed writing, you'd have a hard time understanding how to generalize objects into categories. Imagine you are in a culture that doesn't read or write. Someone arrives one day and shows you squares and circles on a piece of paper. You might say you see a house, a plate, or a moon—all things that look like squares or circles. But, you wouldn't say that you see two "shapes" because "shapes" is a category that squares and circles belong to. Writing and reading allow your brain to put thoughts out in front of it and think about those thoughts differently. It is the invention of literacy that helped humans develop logic which in turn helps us to generalize our thoughts.[28]

What if books also build on themselves? Not only do some books have sequels, so that a single story continues developing, nonfiction books have editions, so they can be updated with new information. Spreading and updating new information allows people to develop new ideas and create new technologies. Without books there'd be no computers, internet, or video games!

ACTIVITY
Remember and Tell a Story

Read or write a short story. Then try to memorize it. Once you think you have it, go to a parent, sibling, or friend and recite what you can remember. No notes! Was it difficult to remember without reading it?

ANNE MANGEN,
READING RESEARCHER

Reading is good for you. Reading as little as six minutes a day can reduce stress, help your brain function as you get older, and help the prevention of Alzheimer's.[29] But what if there's a difference between reading an electronic book and a paper book?

Anne Mangen, lead researcher on a reading study at Stavanger University in Norway, found that "the haptic and tactile feedback of a Kindle does not provide the same support for mental reconstruction of a story as a print pocket book does."[30] That means that if you can't feel an electronic book in the same way you can feel a paper book, you probably won't remember the book as well as you could.

Other studies suggest that a reader's inability to control the text physically (physically turn pages, bend pages, or write directly on the pages) results in a reduced long-term memory of what was read.[31]

What if You Lived in a Floating City?

Throughout history, humans have been confined to landmasses when establishing permanent living settlements. But what if that's all about to change? What if humans took to the sea, not just to traverse it, but to settle it?

If the Seasteading Institute[32] accomplishes its goal of creating the first permanent cities at sea, your future could involve living with water flowing underneath your feet and land being something you see off on the horizon.

> "I would buy a bunch of swimsuits and water tubes to play with if it was [on] water."
> —Kelly, Findley Elementary, age 10

Originally, the Seasteading Institute envisioned these floating cities establishing themselves as sovereign countries; however, it's shifted its vision to making them new cities for existing countries.[33] These micro cities would be built on movable, floating platforms, each of which could accommodate up to 270 residents.[34]

Sound like an impossible idea? From the perspective of the Seasteading Institute:

Over thirty million people a year already visit floating cities in the form of cruise ships. These ships provide water, food, power, service staff and safety from the waves at a cost as low as $60 per night. There are also 1,500 oil and gas platforms in US waters alone.[35]

These floating cities would simply combine the amenities and engineering of cruise ships and oil platforms to provide people with a permanent life at sea.

> "I would move our city somewhere else using paddles."
> —Stephen, Findley Elementary, age 9
>
> "I would love it because I will be able to find myself in a different place every day."
> —Olivia, Findley Elementary, age 9

ACTIVITY
Design Your Own Floating City

Imagine you've been asked to design a floating city for yourself and 269 of your closest friends. While you wouldn't be permanently cut off from ever visiting land again, there are some things you probably wouldn't want to live long without. What kinds of shops, services, and amenities would you want on your floating city? What kinds of things should you include to make land lovers want to give up their lives as they know them and settle permanently in your sea city?

> "It would be amazing if we could live on a floating city. We could go swimming so often, and we wouldn't have to go to a pool, and instead of going to the pet store for a fish, you could just catch one. And fishermen don't have to go to the lake."
> —Philippa, Oxford Elementary, age 9

PETER THIEL, MONEY GIVER

What if there were someone who would pay you *not* to go to school? And what if that's not a "what if" but a "what is"? Not only did billionaire Peter Thiel cofound the Seasteading Institute[36], he also created the Thiel Fellowship, a $100,000 award given every year to twenty people under twenty years old. One of the requirements to be eligible to receive the award is that the applicant has to drop out of or not go to college. Instead, that person works with visionary mentors to help turn dream projects into realities.[37]

"We would run out of food and everything."
—Conner, Columbia Elementary, age 11

"You would use boats as cars. They would use chocolate syrup in the bathtub instead of water. They would only eat water."
—Conner, Columbia Elementary, age 11

"I would train jellyfish to let me ride them everywhere."
—Edward, Columbia Elementary, age 11

"That would be amazing, and I could ride baby harbor seals around town."
—Jake, Columbia Elementary, age 11

"If you lived on a boat, you would probably get sick a lot and would have to be very smart to figure out how to get vitamin C in the water."
—Halle, Columbia Elementary, age 11

"It would be really cool, and I can snorkel with the plankton."
—Luke, Columbia Elementary, age 11

"We would sink by now, and how would we build new buildings? How are we going to grow crops? Plus a shark might bump into us."
—Aidan, Columbia Elementary, age 10

What if the State of California Became Six Different States?

Ever since August 21, 1959, the United States has been a union of fifty states. But what if that number increased? And what if that number went up without the United States having to invade another country? What if a state like California were to transform from  a single state into six different states? Sound crazy? Not to several people in California. In the fall of 2014, Californians voted on an initiative that would have led the way to divide California into the states of Jefferson, West California, Silicon Valley, Central California, North California, and South California.[38] But it sounded crazy enough to enough people for the ballot initiative to be defeated.

Why on earth would anyone suggest dividing up an existing state into multiple states? Lifelong California resident Tim Draper, the billionaire behind the Six Californias idea, said he "came to the conclusion that California is ungovernable."[39] His idea is to mimic the success of start-ups that spring up in his native Silicon Valley and have each new state run—and compete with each other—as if they were start-up companies.[40] According to the organization Draper formed to push his plan forward, Six Californias, the goal is "to create six states with more local, responsive, efficient and representative governments."[41]

ACTIVITY
Split Your State

Take a look at your state or province. Could you divide it up into multiple states or provinces? Where would you draw the new boundaries? What criteria would you use to group territories—geography, education, industry, etc.?

TIM DRAPER, HERO ENTREPRENEUR

Tim Draper's belief in the entrepreneurial spirit doesn't end with his desire to turn state governments into start-ups. He's also created Draper University of Heroes. The Draper University of Heroes is different from most universities because, instead of students taking classes and earning majors in a wide variety of subjects and fields, students receive a single, immersive experience that prepares them to become entrepreneurs.[42]

What if the South Had Won the Civil War?

The American Civil War was the deadliest war in American history.[43] It was much more than a clash of blades and bullets—it was a clash of ideologies. In the end, the Union was preserved, and the country evolved into the country it is today. But what if it had ended differently? What if the Confederacy had won the war?

Of course, it's impossible to say exactly what the United States would look like today if the Union had lost the Civil War, but that hasn't kept historians and writers from imagining how things might have played out. In 1960, MacKinlay Kantor wrote an article in *Look* magazine that he would later publish as a novel called *If the South Had Won the Civil War*. In it, Kantor speculated that Lincoln would still be assassinated and that slavery would still be abolished, but the two countries would exist separately until, eventually, they reunited in 1960.[44]

Another Civil War "What Iffer" was Winston Churchill. In his essay contribution to the 1931 book *History Rewritten*, Churchill imagined the United States if the Confederacy had won the battle of Gettysburg and then went on to win the war. In his imagination, not only did the Confederacy win the American Civil War but this outcome eventually helped prevent the first World War.[45]

COLONEL JEFFERSON F. JONES, AMERICAN ROYALTY

The United States prides itself on being a pillar of democracy. So how is it there was once a kingdom on its soil? When the Civil War tore the United States apart, with states having to choose sides, the Missouri state government declared its support of the Union, but many of its citizens had Southern sympathies. In particular, the people of Callaway County (in a region of the state still known today as Little Dixie[46]) were staunch supporters of the South.

When word got out that Union troops were marching toward Callaway County, Colonel Jefferson F. Jones, of Callaway County, assembled all the men he could find who weren't already off fighting in the war to defend the county. They had nowhere near enough troops to successfully fight off the Union army, so they created an illusion instead. Jones had his men chop down trees and paint the logs black to look like cannons and light multiple campfires at night to make their forces appear formidable. The ruse worked. Jones was able to secure a cease-fire agreement between the United States and Callaway County. Out of their immense pride for their tiny county standing up against mighty US Army, the people of Callaway County proclaimed their county the Kingdom of Callaway County—a label they continue to use today.[47]

What if France Hadn't Helped America in the American Revolutionary War?

The American Revolutionary War is also referred to as the War of Independence because it was fought by the British Colonies in North America against Great Britain in an attempt to gain their independence. The rebel colonies won and grew into what is today the United States of America. There are countless stories and songs that have survived from the war into today. Much of the cultural identity associated with modern-day Americans is tied to the idea of thirteen underdog colonies standing up against the biggest, baddest empire on the planet . . . and winning!

> "I still think we would win."
> —Carter, Columbia Elementary, age 11

But what if we're forgetting to include a crucial fact about the victory? What if the American Revolution would not have turned out the way it did without a little help from some French friends? What if the War of Independence were fought (or won) alone?

> "We would have probably lost the war. We would be under control by the opposing country, and we would not be the United States!"
> —Ceara, Findley Elementary, age 10

The French and British had been bitter enemies for decades before the Revolutionary War began in 1776. A little more than a decade before, in 1763, Britain defeated France in the Seven Years' War. As a result, France lost most of its North American territory. The rebel leaders leveraged France's bitterness against the British to negotiate a deal with France that brought the colonists weapons, ammunition, uniforms, troops, and naval support to help them fight the British.

28

In particular, French assistance played a vital role in getting the British to finally surrender at Yorktown in 1781.[48]

BENJAMIN FRANKLIN, POP STAR DIPLOMAT

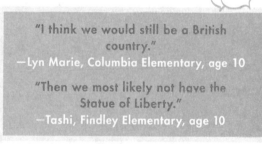

What if one of the most important people in winning the American Revolutionary War spent much of the war thousands of miles away from the nearest battle? It's debatable whether the United States could have defeated the British without French help. It's also debatable whether the United States could have secured French assistance without the help of Benjamin Franklin.

Benjamin Franklin was such a personality that he was able to capture France's imagination to the extent that the country stamped his face on everything it could, such as rings, watches, and medallions. Everyone wanted to wear a Benjamin. He was such a trendsetter that women even started styling their hair after the fur cap he wore. From a purely historical standpoint, it was the American victory over the British at the Battle of Saratoga that tipped the French into lending their

"I think we would still be a British country."
—Lyn Marie, Columbia Elementary, age 10

"Then we most likely not have the Statue of Liberty."
—Tashi, Findley Elementary, age 10

support to the colonies' cause. But it's hard to deny the role the power of Franklin's popularity played in persuading the French to pledge support.[49]

What if Poland Had Joined Germany in 1939?

When Nazi Germany invaded Poland in September 1939, it kicked off a world war that would not only bring its ultimate downfall but the destruction of more land, lives, and property than any war before it.[50] But what if, rather than resisting the Nazis advancing on its borders, Poland had joined them? This is what Hitler would have preferred.[51]

In *The Storm of War: A New History of the Second World War*, Andrew Roberts walked readers through a scenario in which Poland joined forces with the Nazis instead of putting up a month-long resistance, only to be the first domino to fall in a six-year world war. If Germany invading Poland was the first domino, Britain and France declaring war against Germany in response was the second. Roberts believed that Britain and France would not have had any reason to declare war if Poland hadn't been invaded. This would have allowed Germany to invade the Soviet Union with all of its forces, instead of dividing them between an eastern and a western front. The Soviet Union, on the other hand, would likely have had to have divided its forces between the Germans invading in the east and the Japanese invading in the west. Likewise, with the Japanese attacking the Soviet Union from the west, the Japanese wouldn't have attacked Pearl Harbor, thereby keeping the United States out of the war. The result would have been an alliance of Germany, Poland, and Japan fighting—and defeating—a solitary Soviet Union.[52]

The victory would have given them control of a territory similar to that of the Mongol Empire at its height. What they could have done to the rest of the world after that would have been truly terrifying.

JOSEPH STALIN,
MR. BAD-GUY-AND-US-ALLY

What if an ally of the United States in World War II was just as evil as Adolf Hitler? Typically, Hitler is the runaway winner for the title of Worst Human Ever. But what if he was not the clear-cut choice for this infamous title? What if one of the United States' strongest allies in World War II was truly the evilest person to ever live?

Hitler's atrocities are well known, but did you know that Soviet leader Joseph Stalin had thirty thousand members *of his own army* executed just to make sure nobody opposed his authority? He then had everyone who knew about the executions—that's right—executed.[53]

Not only was Stalin responsible for the mass execution of roughly ten million more people than Hitler (Stalin killed forty million[54] to Hitler's thirty million[55]), he was also quoted as saying: "Ideas are more powerful than guns. We would not let our enemies have guns—why should we let them have ideas?"[56]

What if the Internet Were Never Created?

Since the birth of human communication (in other words, since the birth of humans), we've been searching for better and better ways to talk to each other quickly and in synchrony (at the same time).[57] In the winter of 1790, Claude Chappe and his brothers built their first prototype telegraphs.[58] These communication tools could be used to send messages across long distances by having operators look at far off towers with swinging arms. The position of the arms corresponded to letters in the alphabet. Give the signal for a letter with one of the towers; someone a long way away looks out of their own tower, sees the letter, and marks it down. This goes on until the receiving tower has all of the letters and therefore the message. If the message is going to another tower in a line of towers, then the receiving operator has to use their own tower's arms to send the message. Then, another tower down the line has to look out, see the message, and mark it down. Repeat.

You can imagine how slow and tedious this must have been. And, since this relay system was all based on humans looking out windows at towers in the distance, weather could ruin the cross-country communication. This was the beginning of the internet: weird signal towers scattered around France. As time progressed, so did our communications inventions. Chappe invented codebooks so users could

> "Without the internet, life would not be proceeding as fast and efficiently as it is."
> —Garrett, Battle High School, age 16

> "Many people will suffer from their lack of information."
> —Conner, Battle High School, age 15

CLAUDE CHAPPE'S VISUAL TELEGRAPHS

encode their messages into something shorter for cost and privacy. For example, Chappe might send *ABDS* on a visual telegraph, which could mean "Isn't Napoleon kind of short?" This was the real power of visual telegraphs and, starting in the 1830s, electric telegraphs.[59] The inventors and users had created a sort of language, patterns of visual and auditory cues and symbols, for sending and receiving messages. That's exactly what the internet is.

Working at CERN (a research laboratory where scientists study the structure of the universe by smashing elementary particles together), in 1989, Tim Berners-Lee created a language for computers to talk to each other. That language became what we know as the internet. We now have a global communications system where if you can get to a connected device, you can learn and do almost anything. You can send messages almost instantly, watch cat videos, do research for homework, and learn how to build rockets.

> "I'd play Pokemon all the time with all my friends."
> —John Ryan, Battle High School, age 15

But if something were to have stopped its creation, where do you think we'd be today? How much harder would it be to solve global problems or even think about things on the other side of the world? What would we do for fun?

ACTIVITY
Day without Connectivity

Your challenge—if you're brave enough to accept it—is to go an entire day without connectivity. That means no internet, no smartphones, no Xbox Live, and no tablets. Whatever will you do? In your journal, write out how you plan to spend your day of no connectivity and then, after the day is over, how you did spend your day. What was it like? What did you plan to do? What did you do?

TECHNICAL CORNER
The Internet

When you type an address into your browser or when an application you're using picks up data from its servers (a server is just another computer), what happens behind the scenes?

Everything connected to the internet has an address—kind of like how everywhere that gets mail has an address. Your application sends a request to the device it's on, saying, "Hey, you! I want to go look at something at XYZ address." Your device says, "Will do! One moment." It talks to what is called a DNS. A DNS is a server that has a bunch of address information. So, if you are looking for "google.com," a DNS will respond with the internet address for Google. That way, your device knows where to send more requests.

Think about it this way: if you're sending a letter to your friend, you need to know where your friend lives before you can send the letter. So, you could ask your parents "where does my friend live"? They'll let you know so you can label your letter and send it off.

Now that your device has the address to send the request your app had, your device breaks the message down into small packets. Each of these gets sent out to the internet with a destination address. Back to the physical letter example: imagine that when you're sending your letter, the post office makes you cut your letter up into ten-word chunks, each with its own envelope, each marked with your friend's address. That's what happens when internet-connected devices talk to each other—they break up messages into smaller packets and send them all.

The internet is a network of networks. Look at a spiderweb sometime. It has connected strings that go all over the place. That's what the internet looks like: a bunch of crazily connected strings. As your packets go out onto the internet, they get transferred around and around, until they reach their destination. Just like small post offices send letters to larger hubs, which in turn send your letters to other hubs, and eventually to your friend's local hub, then to your friend's door; the internet does the same, routing messages through local, regional, and then local hubs.

When your messages get received by the server, it reads them and decides if it wants to send something back. If it does, then a new message gets created and sent back through the spiderweb of networks until it hits the device you're using. Your device notifies your application, saying, "Hey there! I just got this back for you." Your application then does whatever it needs to with the information, maybe showing you a web page or updating its memory.

Back to physical mail. When your friend gets all of those messages from you, he or she has to put them back together to read your letter. Then, if you asked your friend to answer a question for you, he or she will need to write a response letter, cut it up, and send all the messages through the mail, all the way through the system until the messages arrive at your house to be read by you.[60]

What if There Were No Stories?

Why do you enjoy stories? To have fun? To laugh? To be scared? To imagine? Or just to relax enough to fall asleep? People love stories for all of those reasons and more. But have you ever wondered how stories got their start?

Many of the stories we read today were built from stories of the past. The more you read, the more you'll discover that certain characters and plots are very similar across many stories. For example, what if Harry Potter and Katniss Everdeen have a lot more in common than you realize?

Some even believe that every story we read is, more or less, the same story, just told in different ways. What's the story that's being repeated? Change. In a happy story, a funny story, a scary story, or a sad story, the main character always goes through significant changes by the end. People who study stories believe this is to reflect the changes we go through in life. Reading these stories can then prepare us for the changes we face.

What if stories are life? What if your life is a story (and you're the hero!)?

ACTIVITY
A Hero's Journey

Below is a list of the typical stages heroes go through during a story. Think of your favorite story. Then read the list, pausing at each stage to think about how your story's main character experienced each stage. Can you think of an example for each stage? Now think of another story and main character and see if you can do it again. Can you start to see that many stories we enjoy could be considered the same story?

1. The Ordinary World: Stories usually start by showing the hero in a mundane or unsatisfying world. The hero will often possess some characteristic or ability that sets him or her apart—maybe even making the character uncomfortably different—from those around him or her.

2. Call to Adventure: Something happens in this ordinary world to shake things up. The hero is forced to realize that change is coming . . . and an adventure is about to begin.

3. Refusal of the Call: Even though the coming change is obvious and inevitable, the hero makes one last attempt to refuse the adventure, to stay home or not leave what's familiar. He or she fears the unknown ahead and may even have a friend or family member warning about leaving.

4. Meeting a Mentor: One of the first occurrences during a hero's adventure is the hero meeting a mentor, or guide. This person is typically much older than the hero and often possesses great intelligence and magical or supernatural abilities. The mentor also gives the hero equipment, training, or advice for his or her adventure.

5. Crossing into the Unknown: This is when the hero completely leaves the place, people, or situation that was familiar and goes to where the people, places, and rules are very strange and different.

6. Allies and Enemies: Once in this new world of the unknown, the hero encounters other people who then become his or her allies or enemies for the course of the adventure.

7. Fear and Death: At some point along his or her adventure, a hero comes close to death or must confront his or her greatest fear.

8. Reward: After overcoming this great fear, or escaping his or her death, the hero is rewarded. Often, this is an object or treasure. The hero shows great joy, and others might celebrate this achievement, but the adventure is not over.

9. The Return: Once the hero has his or her reward, it's time to return home. The hero now begins the journey from this new world back to the place where he or she is from.

10. Rebirth: During the hero's return, he or she must now use what was learned along the adventure (and possibly the reward acquired) to overcome one more obstacle (often facing death again). But this time he or she is more prepared to face the challenge and appears to be a new person as a result.

11. Return with the Reward: The hero is now home—or where he or she was before leaving on the adventure—a transformed person. The hero is like a person living in two worlds: back to what is familiar but with the learning obtained from something new. This allows the hero a new freedom. All may not be awesome, but the hero has changed and is ready for new challenges and adventures.

JOSEPH CAMPBELL, LUKE SKYWALKER'S OTHER FATHER

The hero's journey is a concept advanced by anthropologist Joseph Campbell in his book *The Hero with a Thousand Faces*. It was this book (and Campbell's work studying and connecting the myths and stories of humans across the earth and across the history of humanity on it) that guided George Lucas in his writing of *Star Wars*.[61] Lucas said, "I consider him [Campbell] a mentor. He was an amazing scholar and an amazing person. When I started doing *Star Wars*, I reread *Hero with a Thousand Faces*."[62]

Campbell also left several suggestions on how anyone can live life like a hero. Here are two:

"Life is without meaning. You bring the meaning to it. The meaning of life is whatever you ascribe it to be. Being alive is the meaning."[63]

"A hero is someone who has given his or her life to something bigger than oneself."[64]

What if the Future Never Comes?

Implantable memories. Nanobots. Computers that think for themselves. Robot friends. An ability to change our genetic code. Flying cars or cars without drivers. People who never get sick. All these things are said to be waiting for us in the future.

But what if that future never comes? What if all the technology we have right now is going to stay the same? What if we don't create anything new but have to just keep using what we have?

Would you be happy with what we have? Would you still want a faster computer, a faster phone, a healthier life? How do you think society would respond to everything stopping?

ACTIVITY
Happy/Sad List

If technology stopped changing, what would you be happy to not have to experience in the future? What would you be sad about never being able to experience? Write your list in your journal!

KEVIN KELLY, STEVEN JOHNSON, AND RAY KURZWEIL, TECHNOLOGICAL DETERMINISTS

There's this idea called *technological determinism*. You might have heard your parents say something was "determined to happen." That means that whatever they're talking about was going to happen no matter what (or mostly no matter what). It doesn't matter if, when going down a road, a person chooses the left path or the right path, this thing (whatever the thing is) is destined to be—it's determined to happen. *Technological determinism* is determinism related to technology.

Kevin Kelly, Steven Johnson, and Ray Kurzweil all believe in this. Coincidentally, they also all write about technology. They each think that, given a certain setup, both organisms and technology will evolve in certain patterns. This might seem strange if you've heard that evolution is a whole bunch of random happenings. Evolution certainly has a random component to it, but it also has a less random part.

Think about it this way: if you're in a sandwich shop, you can order a whole bunch of different sandwiches made up of various ingredients. There are a limited number of ingredients, and, thus, there are only so many combinations of ingredients you can have to make a sandwich. Some combinations are pretty terrible, like mayo, mustard, and pepper. There's not really a sandwich there, and it's kind of hard to eat. But you could put some bread around those and add turkey, lettuce, and cheese. Now you have a sandwich. Sweet! Some people have an allergic reaction to an ingredient in bread, so they can't use bread to hold their sandwich together. This is where a little bit of technological determinism comes in . . . or would it be sandwich determinism? Large lettuce leaves could be wrapped around your other sandwich innards. Using lettuce as a wrap is somewhat determined. Lettuce has certain properties: it's big, it's flexible, it's found at sandwich shops, and it isn't greasy when you hold it. These properties make it a popular choice when you can't use bread. It is a choice that *will* happen when non-bread people need a good sandwich.

Why are we talking about technological determinism here? We're talking about it because even if there is a horrible, terrible, no-good world disaster, there are some things that might still be bound to happen.

Kevin Kelly talks about technological determinism in the broad sense of technology where it "extends beyond shiny hardware to include culture, art, social institutions, and intellectual creations of all types."[65] In his view, all of technology obeys some deterministic rules. The only thing we can do through our choices is slow technology's growth but not stop it.[66]

Steven Johnson writes about technology from an ideas-and-innovation perspective. In his view, ideas grow in somewhat set pathways. Similar to the lettuce-instead-of-bread example earlier, our ideas can only grow to their neighboring related ideas (you can't come up with a lettuce-wrapped sandwich if you haven't created the idea of a sandwich yet) and settle into various determined balance points (lettuce and bread both hold other sandwich ingredients well).[67]

Ray Kurzweil largely examines computers and artificial intelligence. There's a famous law in technology called "Moore's Law." It states for every two years that pass, you can pack two times as many transistors on an integrated circuit. Basically, that means that computers get more powerful and faster at a known rate. Well, Kurzweil saw this and wondered about the time before Moore's Law and the time after. He found that computers, for as long as there were computers, have followed this curve of powerfulness and speediness. And beyond that, he proposed that computers in the future are determined to follow this. So far, he's been right.[68]

What if the First Olympics Were a Science Competition Instead of an Athletic One?

Can you imagine how different the world would look today if, way back during the time of ancient Greece, people came from all over to compete in science? Sure, science was and is valued, but what if it were celebrated in the same way as sports are?

> "I think the First Olympics would be boring because science is not an energetic subject."
> —Avery, Findley Elementary, age 10

What if, instead of trading cards and wearing jerseys of your favorite sports star, you had a lab coat or a poster of your favorite scientist? And what if scientists made millions of dollars and were featured on television the way our sports stars are?

How do you think schools would look today if we celebrated science as much as sports? Would competitions in which science teams from different schools competed against each other draw large crowds with bands, cheerleaders, and die-hard fans the way school athletic teams do today?

> "There would be stuff like flying cars and time travel."
> —Capone, Oxford Elementary, age 8

Do you think more students would get excited about studying and participating in science-related activities?

Perhaps the biggest question is how different the entire world would look if we had millions of people who were science fanatics instead of sports fanatics. What kinds of advances and new technology would we have today?

If you could play a sport or do a science experiment, which would you choose?

"Science gets so little appreciation by the general public that it gets very little funding and advances much slower than is possible. If people were to get as excited about science and research as they do professional sports, then they could help fund progress and be a part of progress."
—Landon, Columbia Elementary School, age 10

"People would perfect the cure to cancer to win a gold metal. Or find the cure to Ebola."
—Elise, Findley Elementary, age 10

"Nerds would be more respected."
—Francesca, Findley Elementary, age 10

"Then all the athletic people would be poor, and the smart people would be rich."
—Lucas, Findley Elementary, age 10

"I think there would be a lot more scientists, and we probably would have made a lot more discoveries."
—Madyson, Columbia Elementary, age 11

"I think if the Olympics were a scientific competition that young boys and girls would want to try new things and experiment more often. It would lessen the popularity of sports."
—Maximum, Columbia Elementary, age 11

"Then no one would care about sports very much. We might study athletics instead of science."
—Calliope, Columbia Elementary, age 10

"Then Rome would know a lot about the science they learned from the Olympics, and the first manned rocket would be launched in the 1800s!"
—Schuyler, Columbia Elementary, age 11

What if Electricity Could Travel through the Air?

You know all about Wi-Fi and how great it is that you can access the internet without wires, but, at the end of the day, you still have to plug your devices into a wall socket to give them the juice to work wirelessly. What if you could power up anywhere, even where there are no walls?

This isn't a new thought. Since the dawn of electricity, people have been frustrated by wires. In fact, one of the great pioneers in electricity, Nikola Tesla, had a vision of free, wireless electricity for the entire world . . . over a hundred years ago! At the beginning of the twentieth century, Tesla started building the Wardenclyffe Tower (aka Tesla Tower) that would have provided electricity to cities, buildings, and homes wirelessly and inexpensively.[69] But the cost of finishing the tower became too much. Construction stopped, Tesla had a nervous breakdown, and we've used wires to transmit electricity for more than one hundred years.[70] Even though we may have missed our chance to have wireless electricity over a hundred years ago, scientists and inventors are hard at work making it a reality in the near future. There's a very good chance you'll be using 100 percent wireless devices before you know it.

ACTIVITY
Wireless History

But what if we did have wireless technology for the past century? How would this have affected other technological developments? Imagine if people could have had power wherever they went.

Do you think things like computers and the internet may have been developed years—if not decades—earlier? What if your great-grandparents had grown up with smartphones? What kinds of devices do you think you'd have today?

Write an alternative history, a short description of what the world could have been like. You can even draw some of the things we could have had by now. How would the world be different?

NIKOLA TESLA, SUPER-SCIENTIST-INVENTOR

Nikola Tesla came to the United States in 1884 to work with Thomas Edison.[71] He spent his life inventing. He helped push alternating current (the type of electricity in your house). He invented new types of motors. He invented the first radio receivers and, thus, was one of the main people to invent wireless electronic communications. He also invented hydroelectric power.[72]

Unfortunately, Tesla didn't always get as much recognition as he should have because other people took advantage of his kindness. He was reclusive and spent his time pursuing scientific discoveries, so he never had a spouse or children. Ultimately, he died alone in a New York City hotel from a blood clot in his heart. Over 2,000 scientists, engineers, politicians, and friends attended Tesla's funeral to pay their respects and say goodbye to a greatly respected inventor.[73]

TECHNICAL CORNER
Wireless Power

Wireless power works by sending out what're called electromagnetic waves. These waves have electrical and magnetic components that work together. In fact, there are a whole bunch of these kinds of waves you might already know about: radio waves (waves that carry the signals from radio stations), microwaves (the waves inside your microwave oven), infrared waves (the waves heat gives off), all the light you see (visible light waves), ultraviolet waves (the ones that give you a sunburn!), and x-rays (waves that doctors use to see your broken bones).

Each of these waves carries energy, even if you can't see it. When one of these waves matches the pattern of something else, its energy can transfer. For example, microwaves move in a way that resonates with water. Food heats up in your microwave because the energy from the waves it sends out gets picked up by the water in your food. The waves make the molecules in the water move more (which is what heat is). But your microwave can't pick up radio signals because it doesn't match that pattern, just like your radio can't heat your food. But, if you have a radio, it can pick up radio waves.

There are a few ways to send power wirelessly. One way is using simple induction. Imagine you are standing close to two friends. Jane is on your right, and Joe is on your left. Joe pushes you toward Jane. Then Jane pushes you toward Joe. This keeps happening, and you keep moving left and right. That's induction! Jane and Joe are using the energy in their arms to move you. You pick up their energy when you move. If you had two wires that were close to each other, you could send power to one by continuously switching the direction of electricity in the other.

Part 2
People

People. Can't live with them, can't live without them. And you are one, so what if there were a way to get the most out of being one? People come with all different sizes, backgrounds, perspectives, interests, and futures. It's remarkably easy to act as if you're the only person on the planet. But what if learning how to better understand those other people with which you share this big, blue marble hurtling through space would not only make the world we all share a better place but also would make you a better person?

We're all connected through space and time, but how much do we really know about each other? What if, by asking and exploring questions together about who people are, we can also boost what people can do? What if, in understanding people as a whole, you can also develop a deeper understanding of the person that is you?

Whether exploring questions about the length of our lives, the powers we have and how we should use those powers, or what our roles are when we interact together, there's a lot to talk about when it comes to the potential of people.

What if the future is a brighter place when we're all shining there together?

What if People Lived for Only One Day?

Mayflies, a species of fly, live for a few hours to a day after they reach adulthood.[1] Their experience of the world is just one, a small sliver of what you see.

What if you only lived for one day?

If you knew your life would last only from the time you were born until the time you fell asleep, how would you spend your day? Would you spend it having as much fun as possible? Or would you rush to make as big of a difference in the world as you could?

How would a one-day lifespan affect the way you viewed and treated others? Would you be like, "Out of my way! I've only got one day to live—and it's almost over!"? Or would you spend as much time with friends and family as you could?

> "Just like flies, they would run around like crazy trying desperately to procreate and leave a legacy of their being behind."
> —Kate, Battle High School, age 15

What about your view of the future? When you think about how little humans consider the future now, when our existence can span up to a century, where would our focus be if our time would be up in twenty-four hours? How would we treat the planet? How would we treat each other?

ACTIVITY
Single-Day Planner

What would you do if you had just today? Rush through your day, filling it with as much action as you could in the hopes of creating "meaning"? Or would you slow it down and soak in every last second of your day? Fill out a daily schedule for a single day. For each of the twenty-four hours in a day, write out what you would do.

ACTIVITY
Record a Day of Your Life

Choose an upcoming day. On that day, take pictures, record audio, collect artifacts, and make a bunch of written entries that capture everything that happens. Put what you can in your journal. How would you feel if that were the only day you were going to be alive? Would you be satisfied?

"People wouldn't be so judgmental, and they would take advantage of their limited time and resources."
—Leslie, Battle High School, age 16

"If people only lived for one day, people would be forced to cram life experiences into the twenty-four hours that they would be alive. Instead of having years to basically waste, every second of that day would count significantly more, so time would become the most valuable thing in the world."
—Dillon, Battle High School, age 16

"I would still sleep for half of it. The other half I would eat. I would question if I could do both at once and then be dead never knowing if I could."
—Charlie, Battle High School, age 15

"We would all have to live on Venus where one day is equal to about 223 Earth days."
—Andrew, Battle High School, age 15

What if We Could Be Young Forever?

Every year, you get a little older, until one day, well, you don't. You die. It happens. Ideas about what happens after we die are as plentiful as there are people on the planet. But what if you didn't have to wonder about what's next? What if you never died? What if you could live forever? What if everyone lived forever? What if when you aged, you didn't get physically older?

How do you think longer lives would change society? Right now, people are born, they grow, they get a job and go to work, and then they retire. But if we could live forever, there'd be no need to retire. We could work forever! Sound like fun?

If you could live forever, you could also learn anything you wanted and pursue as many interests as you wanted. What if you could become a doctor, a musician, an athlete, an astronaut, and more instead of choosing just one? You could play every video game. You could watch every movie. You could travel to every country!

But what if you weren't the only one who was living forever?

It would seem that we would need to do something about all the people being born. In 2012, 451 babies were born every minute![2] How do we feed all those people? Will there be enough room for everyone? What changes might we have to make in order to make sure the planet is prepared for people living forever?

ACTIVITY
Write a Letter to Yourself in the Future

Write a letter to yourself five hundred years in the future. What are some of the things you're doing and thinking right now that you want to make sure you don't forget after you're five hundred years old?

AUBREY DE GREY, CHIEF SCIENCE OFFICER, SENS RESEARCH FOUNDATION

Aubrey de Grey used to be a computer scientist. Then he realized that something is killing humans more than anything else: aging. He changed career paths to start researching life-extension—how we could live drastically longer and healthier lives.

[Life-extension] will empower us, both individually and as a society. The psychological impact of seeing our loved ones decline, and of knowing that sometime in the future the same thing will happen to us, is so huge that our only defense (for most of us . . .) is to ignore it. When we no longer have that, we will be far more able to aim high, in our personal and professional lives and as a society: we will believe that we can succeed against our other big challenges too, whether it be climate change, war, or pandemics.[3]

TECHNICAL CORNER
How Do We Die?

Loads of processes keep us alive. Our hearts pump our blood. Our intestines remove nutrients from what we eat. Our immune system fights off bacteria, viruses, fungi, and parasites. Our nerves send command and sense signals all around our body. It's pretty amazing!

Just like when your parents' car runs for a while and builds up damage, so do we. After enough damage, we will get a disease. And when things break down all the way, we die. Researchers like Aubrey de Grey are trying to combat each of the following causes of damage so we might never get that disease that kills us.

1. Cell loss, cell atrophy: Cells die too quickly.
2. Division-obsessed cells: Cells like dividing themselves in two too much. This is what many tumors are.
3. Death-resistant cells: Cells don't die quickly enough. All cells die, but resistant cells can cause problems too.
4. Mitochondrial mutations: Mitochondria help provide the energy to cells. If they are damaged then cells can't make the energy they need.
5. Intracellular junk: Cells have picked up too much waste. As the body cleans itself, that waste has to be transported to waste areas, but cells can get damaged if the body can't get rid of its waste.
6. Extracellular junk: Similar to waste in a cell, this waste is outside of the cell and damages the body.
7. Extracellular matrix stiffening: The stiffening of the tissue that connects all of your cells. If it can't move like it needs to, your body gets damaged.[4]

What if Politicians Were Kids?

When was the last time a politician asked you what you think? Have people from your city, state, and federal governments ever asked you about how things should be run?

We're guessing they've probably never asked you. Well, what if kids had a greater voice in government? Sure, politicians might have more experience than kids with certain matters. It is one of the reasons voters vote for certain candidates. But while having experience in a topic can be really useful to thinking about that topic, it also can make your thinking more limited. That's why people with only a little bit of experience can contribute a great deal to a conversation. A person with less experience isn't guided by (what could be) faulty ways of thinking about a problem.

Kids have a unique perspective. You solve problems all the time and look at the world differently than older people. What do you think would happen if more kids were in government? Do you think kids should run for office? Do you think politicians should talk to you?

"Children would be more open-minded and hopefully would not have predetermined judgments. To let the children run the government on their own, however, would probably be a bad thing. Adults still need to bring their wisdom and experience to the table and still be the major guiding force within the government. But the fresh opinions and out-of-the-box thinking that children would bring is very important and needs to be a bigger part of government."
—Madi, Battle High School, age 15

ACTIVITY
Write to a Politician

Your representatives are the people who make
decisions for you in government, people
at the city, state, and federal levels.
Here's the activity: write a letter to
one of your representatives. First, find
their email or mailing address online.
Then, write a letter telling that person
what you worry about and how you
might go about changing it. Also,
make sure you say that you'll
be voting in future elections.
Politicians are more likely to do
something for people who will vote
for them. Hopefully he or she will write
back!

"I'm sure there would be a lot
less drama."
—Ben, Battle High School, age 17

"There would be a lot more
compassion in the world. As
people age, they are shaped by the
limitations they've seen in the world.
Kids would be much better at solving
the problems because kids are more
creative, and they would actually
be more focused on solving the
problems of the world, rather than
creating more of them."
—Dillon, Battle High School, age 16

What if There Were No Holidays?

What? No holidays? That was the case for the first ninety-four years of the United States. It wasn't until June 28, 1870, that the first federal holiday law was enacted. This law officially made New Year's Day, Independence Day, and Christmas holidays in the United States. It also opened the door for the establishment of other holidays.[5]

There have been over one thousand holidays proposed to become federal holidays since the fun began in 1870, but only eleven have made the cut.[6] Can you name all of them?

It wasn't until George Washington's birthday joined the party in 1879 that federal employees got a paid day off. Christopher Columbus may have been one of the first Europeans to land in the Americas, but Columbus Day, established in 1968, was one of the last federal holidays established—until Martin Luther King Jr. Day, the most recent federal holiday, was created back in 1983.

Each holiday has a unique history, but what if Thanksgiving has the craziest?

The first Thanksgiving was when George Washington declared "a day of thanksgiving and prayer" on Thursday, November 26, 1789. But the second Thanksgiving wasn't celebrated until Washington called for another day of thanksgiving over six years later, on February 19, 1795. Abraham Lincoln, fifteen presidents later, thankfully brought an end to the madness of this moveable feast in 1863 and proclaimed the United States would celebrate Thanksgiving once a year on the last Thursday of November. Thanksgiving didn't settle on its present date (the third Thursday of November) until 1941, when President Franklin Roosevelt put it there.

Why did Roosevelt move Thanksgiving Day back a week? To give stores an extra week for Christmas shopping—a decision for which business owners remain thankful today.

ACTIVITY
Your Own Holiday

What if you could make your dream holiday? What would it be about? On what day of the year would this holiday happen, and what sorts of traditions and activities would be involved in this celebration? You already have a birthday, but what if you had a new day with a new theme?

What if You Hibernated?

Sure, you like to sleep in an extra hour or two whenever you can, but what if you slept in an extra six months?! That's how long some hibernating animals sleep. Black bears can go up to one hundred days without eating, drinking, or going to the bathroom![7]

For starters, imagine how hungry you'd be when you woke up after sleeping (and not eating) for many months. This is why hibernating animals spend most of the summer and fall eating to pack on the pounds. Black bears can put on an extra thirty pounds every week before their super long slumber.[8] But bears aren't the only animals that hibernate. There are species of snakes, turtles, lizards, toads, bats, and even shrimp who feel the need for sleep, always in the wintertime.[9] Why not you?

> "I would feel much more energized after hibernation, but life would seem much shorter because we would be sleeping, and time would pass faster."
> —Veronica, Battle High School, age 17

You may not believe it, but human hibernation isn't as crazy as it sounds. It might even be helpful. Scientists have identified a couple genes in humans that might allow us to hibernate, but we'd have to undergo treatment to start. Doctors could add or remove genes, or they could use medicine or environmental factors to allow these genes to express themselves. It's somewhat similar to cooking: when you want your cake to turn out a certain way, you add, remove, and change the amount of ingredients. But, why would a person ever *want* to sleep that long? Perhaps the most

> "I already do."
> —Andrew, Battle High School, age 15

exciting reason for a person to hibernate is space travel. Traveling through space can take a long time. It takes two hundred to three hundred days just to reach Mars![10] Traveling to other interesting places in our universe can take years, if not decades.

How would you use your ability to hibernate? Would you sleep through long trips, boring movies, or entire seasons of the year?

ACTIVITY
Find Your Hibernating Friends

We told you a few species that hibernate. Who else can you find? Start with a little research on the internet or in other books for an animal that hibernates. Then, go to your local zoo and try to find that animal. When you do, take a picture of it (or even with it). Put the picture and a short description of what you've learned in your journal.

"Teens already do that. We sleep as much as we can and eat large quantities. We are only active during the summer because we don't have school."
—Charlie, Battle High School, age 15

What if the Jobs of the Future Were Different?

What do you want to do when you grow up? Be a doctor? A lawyer? How about an astronaut? A factory worker? A construction worker?

What if the job you'll have when you're older doesn't even exist yet? What if you can create your future job? What would it be? What would you do?

One of the wonderful things about technology is that machines can do some jobs humans used to do but didn't enjoy very much. Imagine digging huge ditches out in the blazing sun. Doesn't sound like much fun, huh? Today, we have gigantic machines that can dig thirty-two feet every minute and move more than 2.7 million cubic feet of earth every day![11]

But it's not just moving dirt. Other jobs are slowly becoming obsolete.[12] As computers get smarter, they're able to correct our spelling and grammar. What if we no longer need proofreaders? What if we no longer need teachers?

What, no teachers? Sounds crazy, but there are some people today, like Sugata Mitra, who believe the future of education will be students with computers in a classroom—without a teacher![13]

> "I would ask myself for a raise, and probably only be able to get a new title."
> —Charlie, Battle High School, age 15
>
> "People, including myself, would be much more happy with their lives because they [would have] the power to control their work environment completely."
> —Veronica, Battle High School, age 17

And what about those other careers popular with kids today, like doctors[14] and lawyers[15]? Many futurists believe humans won't be doing those jobs either in the future. Heck, with Google's driverless

59

car[16], you may not even be able to get a job driving a taxi, bus, ambulance, or fire truck.

So, what will you do?

What if today is the time to start thinking about tomorrow? On the bright side, some of the jobs that will be done by machines are jobs must humans didn't want to do in the first place. By having machines do these jobs, humans as a whole can explore new activities. However, people who like jobs done by robots might get forced into jobs less likely to be taken over by machines. Think about the kind of job you want. Do you think it can be replaced by robots? Can you come up with an entirely new job that doesn't exist yet, one that wouldn't be replaced by machines?

> "I would sit, be a professional doodler, and [be a] taste tester."
> —Kate, Battle High School, age 15

Do you love to travel? What if you became a personal tour guide?

Like sports? You could become a personal trainer.

Enjoy cooking? You can bake treats and sell them to the world through an online store.

Are you creative? There's nothing stopping you from creating your art and then using the internet to share it with the world.

What if, in the future, people stop asking other people what work they do for a living and start asking what they enjoy doing for a living?

ACTIVITY
Read This Book, Create a New Job

Many of the entries in this book have futuristic elements. After reading more of the book, come back to this activity and describe a new job based on something you read. Your new job could even be from what you learned while you were doing a different activity. Write it up in your journal and then search the internet for jobs like it. Does it exist yet, or are you the first to describe this job?

What if We All Spoke the Same Language?

In 2014, there were 7,106 different spoken languages, according to Ethnologue,[17] a world language research group. That's a lot of languages. However, 40 percent of the world speaks one (or more) of eight major languages: Chinese, Spanish, English, Hindi, Arabic, Portuguese, Bengali, and Russian.[18] On top of that, many languages are dying out for a multitude of reasons. This leads us to the question: what if we all spoke the same language?

Which language do you think it'd be? This book is printed in English, but English is only the third most popular language (at least at the time we're writing this).[19] Language is highly tied to power and culture. English is powerful because of British expansion and the United States' strong role in world economics.

What about some of the properties of language? English gets kind of greedy. When it finds a word in a different language it likes, English just steals it. For example *anger* comes from Scandinavia, *dance* comes from France, *skeleton* comes from Greece.[20] Look at German. It can putwordstogethertomeannewthings. For example, a person who wears gloves to throw snowballs is a *handschuhschneeballwerfer.*[21]

We also know ideas are tied to our language. If you've ever learned another language, you've probably learned about a few concepts that just don't translate well. Will we lose certain ideas that can only be expressed in one language? Or do you think we'll figure out a way to say these things in a new language?

ACTIVITY
What's in a Good Language?

If you had to build a language, what would be special about it? What would be useful and why? Could you string words together? Could you steal from other languages? Could you add new letters and other symbols? Could you change the way it is written? What would you choose?

L. L. ZAMENHOF, FATHER OF ESPERANTO

Dr. L. L. Zamenhof created Esperanto in 1887 to allow people of different languages the ability to communicate easily with each other without feeling as if they were sacrificing their own cultural identities when speaking. He also designed it to be logical and easy to learn so as many people as possible could use it—not just those who could afford to go to school to learn it.[22] Today, it is estimated that as many as 2 million people speak fluent Esperanto.[23]

What if People Didn't Know Anything?

Knowledge can be defined as "justified, true, belief."[24] So, if you have a thought, and you're wondering if it is knowledge or not, you can ask yourself three questions. (1) Is this thought a belief? (2) Is this thought true? (3) Is this thought justified? If you answer yes to all three, you've got a little nugget of knowledge!

The first question is pretty easy to answer. A *belief* is just a thought that you think is true (regardless of if it is true or false). "I believe the Earth orbits the sun," and "I believe there is a civilization of mole-people at the center of the Earth" are my beliefs if I believe them to be true. Question one: done.

But be careful! The next two questions are harder. Truth doesn't depend on what people think. A thing is either true or false, regardless of whether or not a person believes it to be true or false. (Well, there are a few weird things that do crazy things with logic and quantum mechanics, but we'll leave them out for now.) Anyway, how do you know if something is true or false? You might know it is true if it's a thing you can see (example: these powders explode when lit because when I light them, they explode). You might be able to deduce it is true if the thought is based in logic (example: $1 + 1 = 2$ because that is how math works). You might hear someone you trust say it's true (example: your teacher tells you that America used to have slaves). But how certain are you of any of these things?

This is where we get into justification. To be justified in a belief, you have to have enough evidence that a thing is true with enough reasonableness. So, your teacher tells you that there are mole-people at the center of the Earth. At first you believe her because she tells you other things you know to be true. But later on, you ask other trustworthy people about the mole-people. Turns out they don't think there is anyone down there. You then study geology, you read about how the Earth works, and you learn about the molten core. Now you have more evidence that there is no one, not even mole-people, living at the center of the Earth. You would now be justified in *not* believing what your teacher told you about mole-people because you have more evidence against her statement than for her statement.

How do you make sure your beliefs are properly justified? How do you make sure your beliefs are true? Do the things you "know" stand up to the test? If you are pretty sure about your beliefs, is that really you "knowing"?

ACTIVITY
Test Your Knowledge

In a journal or notebook, write down three things you think you know. Now, go through each of these things and write what your belief is, how you know it is true, and how you are justified in believing it. When you're writing how you know it's true and how you're justified in believing it, don't just say, "My teacher told me." Write out a few sentences about how you know. What other things do you know that lead you to thinking your belief is true?

What if We Got Rid of Cars?

Wherever you live, you probably have many cars around you. America especially likes cars—Ford Motor Company, General Motors Corporation, Chrysler, and others started in America. And there are countless movies and songs that romanticize cars and driving. No wonder America likes cars so much—it's part of the culture!

Jane Jacobs, urban activist and writer, thought that cities (including rural ones) are a balance of two things: city function and transportation.[25] Grocery stores, bookshops, big business buildings, homes—these are all containers of city functions. It's what is happening in the city. Transportation is how we get from one city function container to the next. You can walk, bike, drive a car, take a bus, or fly your blimp—these are all forms of transportation.

> "It would be awesome because you could play baseball or ride your bike in the street."
> —Isaac, Oxford Elementary, age 9
>
> "There would be much more space and there [would] be more buildings, and there wouldn't be as much putrid air."
> —Charlie, Oxford Elementary, age 9

City functions are the places we want to be, though. We don't want to be driving around all day. We want to be hanging out, riding roller coasters, sitting in the park—we want to be *doing* things. So, what if we got rid of cars?

Roads take up a lot of space. But if we didn't have

cars, buses, trucks, or other large vehicles that need that space, we could fill it in with more activities! If we got rid of cars today, we'd certainly have a lot of empty space between buildings (especially where parking lots used to be). Think of all the weirdly shaped buildings we could put between current buildings. Think of all the new activities that could be so much closer to where you live! But would it be harder to get there?

> "If we got rid of cars, then people would be a lot more fit and healthy because they would have to walk everywhere. Also no one would be able to visit faraway places."
> —Emily, Findley Elementary, Age 10

ACTIVITY
You Fill in the Streets

What would you put between our buildings if cars (and similar transportation) just disappeared? Draw two pictures. Your first picture should be of a street including cars, people, and buildings. Then, draw your second picture of the same street but replace all the cars and the roads with new buildings or activities.

JANE JACOBS, URBAN ACTIVIST AND WRITER

Jane Jacobs started as a writer in New York City. For her pieces, she went to different parts of the city for inspiration. Over time, Jacobs learned a lot about the city and eventually wrote *The Death and Life of Great American Cities*. She wrote this as someone who had no formal training in public planning (the study and profession of putting cities together). It is now one of the most important books about cities, and she has affected cities beyond measure.

Jacobs believed that cities are made of all sorts of people, and that buildings and neighborhoods should reflect that. When New York City planners wanted to demolish homes of the poor so a highway could be built, she fought them for a more balanced city. If you have an area of your city with mixed-use buildings (homes, businesses, and shops in the same structure), you might have a city planner who was inspired by Jacobs.[26]

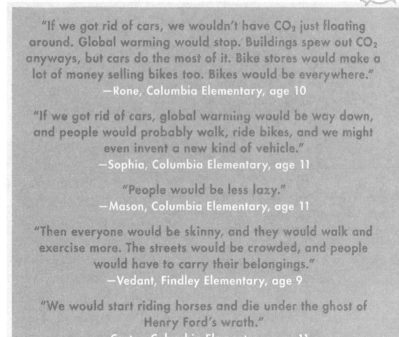

"If we got rid of cars, we wouldn't have CO_2 just floating around. Global warming would stop. Buildings spew out CO_2 anyways, but cars do the most of it. Bike stores would make a lot of money selling bikes too. Bikes would be everywhere."
—Rone, Columbia Elementary, age 10

"If we got rid of cars, global warming would be way down, and people would probably walk, ride bikes, and we might even invent a new kind of vehicle."
—Sophia, Columbia Elementary, age 11

"People would be less lazy."
—Mason, Columbia Elementary, age 11

"Then everyone would be skinny, and they would walk and exercise more. The streets would be crowded, and people would have to carry their belongings."
—Vedant, Findley Elementary, age 9

"We would start riding horses and die under the ghost of Henry Ford's wrath."
—Carter, Columbia Elementary, age 11

What if There Were No Sports?

How would you spend your free time if there were no athletics? What would motivate you to be physically active? Could you still learn the value of teamwork if there were no teams to be a part of? We often think of sports as just a spectacle of winning and losing, but what if there's more to them? What if sports provide people with an outlet to physically exert themselves? Without playing sports, where would all of that energy go? Fighting with each other? That would be awful! Sports also provide us with a distraction from our everyday (sometimes boring) lives. Do you work harder on your homework if you know you get to watch your favorite team play as soon as you're done? Or would you have more time to do your homework if you didn't have the distraction of sports?

> "If there were no sports, society would have to find something else to keep them physically fit, and society would have to find something else to follow and be fans of. Artistic interest might become a social norm, and people might discuss actors, dancers, artists, and writers in place of famous athletes. Maybe scientific interests would flourish. Who knows what would capture our society's attention in place of the worldwide obsession with sports and athleticism?"
> —Madi, Battle High School, age 15

Speaking of getting your work done, sports give us a framework to be competitive in constructive ways. Do you enjoy competing with yourself or against others? If sports didn't exist, how do you think you could develop your competitive edge?

Of course, some people can take sports and competition a little (or way) too far. Do you know people who are a little too in love with winning or like their favorite teams a little too much?

What do you think these people would love if their favorite teams stopped playing?

ACTIVITY
Play Shnorjin

What is shnorjin? We don't know. You haven't created it yet.

Your task is to create a new sport. It has to be something that can be played with one or more people with some goal that can be attained. Write out the rules in your journal and then find a few friends to play with you. If they also have this book, they could create their own version of shnorjin that you could play!

"The arts would be embraced more."
—Leslie, Battle High School, age 16

"Then life wouldn't be as fun."
—John Ryan, Battle High School, age 15

What if You Could Hear and See What Other People Were Thinking?

Do you ever wonder what someone else is thinking? No, we don't mean when someone does something silly and you wonder, "What are you thinking?!" We mean private thoughts, the things you say only to yourself and others say only to themselves.

What would happen if you knew what they were thinking—and they knew what you were thinking?

Doctors, scientists, tech hackers, and entrepreneurs are asking the same questions . . . and they are building tools to look at what people are thinking. If you were to injure your head, your doctor might use an MRI or EEG to figure out exactly what was wrong. These are two tools that let them peer into your thoughts. They can see if you're happy or sad, frustrated or at ease, thinking about a word or image. How would you feel knowing your doctor was seeing your thoughts? We learned about how brains work because of these machines. Researchers are even getting close to being able to record dreams![27]

"That would be helpful for men trying to understand women."
—Charlie, Battle High School, age 15

Well, if machines can see what we're thinking, what if they could do something when you think in certain ways? You could think about watching television, and the television could turn on. Rather than drawing with your hands, you could draw with your brain and a computer. Why draw at all? You could just think of the whole

70

image and have it "print" on a screen. What if you could build 3D structures, like if you were playing with LEGOs or sculpting with clay, but only by using your mind? Research in this area is growing too. The machines you'd use are called brain computer interfaces, or BCIs for short. Pretty neat!

Seeing into people's minds could have downsides too. Your parents would know everything you're thinking. Whoever cooks in your house would know when you think

"I [would] stop acting a fool all the time."
—Ben, Battle High School, age 17

"The world would be a violent place."
—Kate, Battle High School, age 15

their cooking is bad. If you have a secret crush on someone, and that person could read your thoughts, your secret wouldn't be very secret. Nothing would be very secret, would it?

ACTIVITY
With the Power of Your Brain

If you could control objects with your brain, what would you do with that power? Would you become a superhero or a supervillain? Would you use your power for scientific discovery or artistic expression? What about for money or for power? Write in your journal about what you would do.

TECHNICAL CORNER
How to Read Thoughts

Your brain is alive with electricity. When you want to move your arm, an electrical signal is sent from your brain, through your spinal cord, and then into your arm's muscles. Or, when you think a thought, electrical signals get sent to other parts of your brain. If you're trying to remember your friend's face or complete a puzzle, electrical signals again! Weird, right? We don't think about our gooey brains being filled with electricity.

   If a brain scientist put sensors on your scalp, the sensors could measure your brain's electric pulses and how they change. Scientists have been collecting data for many years, and they now have a good idea of which pulses are tied to which thoughts. That means that with enough research, brain scientists can read your thoughts.

"I would be either driven insane or be a billionaire."
—Andrew, Battle High School, age 15

What if Your Community Were More Democratic?

What does it mean to be democratic? Does it mean being a democrat instead of a republican? Nope. *Democratic* comes from *democracy*, which means a type of government where every individual has an equal say in what happens. If your teacher ever asked your class to raise your hands and vote for something, that was probably a temporary democracy! The United States is a *representative democracy*, meaning that everyone elects a few people to represent everyone's ideas in government. Anyway, to be *more democratic* means to give individuals more access to decision-making and actions.

Your community is already somewhat democratic. Officials are elected to local positions. You have a mayor, judges, and someone to make sure all the finances are in order. What if the community voted for even more positions, like each office worker, garbage collector, web designer, and tax preparer? That would be more democratic . . . but you probably don't need everyone to vote on who collects the garbage.

You could also be more democratic by encouraging or allowing more people to vote. Even though many people have the right to vote in elections, they don't always do so. This is one of the reasons why some groups don't get as much representation in government. There are other people who can't vote at all: some crimes take away your right to vote, and some people (probably like you!) are not old enough.

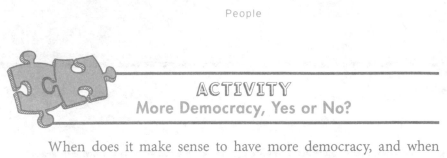

ACTIVITY
More Democracy, Yes or No?

When does it make sense to have more democracy, and when does it make sense to have less? Spend a day jotting down notes in your journal whenever you're making group decisions. Would it make sense to have more or fewer people vote?

What if There Were No School?

No school? Or, at least no more boring parts of school? Awesome!

Wait. What? No school? How would you spend your days? When would you see your friends? What would you learn?

Before we go off and cancel school, what if you took a second and asked yourself what you don't like about school? Is it the tests? Homework? Uncomfortable desks? Boring classes? What if there were solutions to all of those things?

The more we learn about how people learn, the more some schools are moving away from things like long tests, pointless homework, and boring lessons. In fact, more and more schools are starting to include things like toys, 3D printers, and even Minecraft in their classrooms to create more interactive (and effective) learning experiences.

What if, instead of not having school, students like you were able to help design your learning environment and decide the things you studied?

ACTIVITY
Create Your Own Classroom

Draw a picture of your ideal classroom. Include all the things you'd like to have in it to help you learn. Think about how you'd situate different parts of the room. Will you have places for writing, lectures, experiments, books, art, and talking with other students? Will your classroom be inside or outside? How many students are in the class, and are they all the same age?

MALALA YOUSAFZAI, EDUCATION ACTIVIST

If you don't like school, it might sound like fun to all of a sudden not have it. And, sure, maybe "school" isn't the thing that is important to have—education is. It's important to be able to interpret what is going on in the world, how to live with others, and how to learn more. Without any education, we would devolve into apes.

Malala Yousafzai is a Pashtun Pakistani who was shot in the head because she was trying to go to school, trying to get an education. The Taliban, an Islamic fundamentalist terrorist group, targeted Malala because she wrote a blog about how important education is. Malala survived the shooting, and when she recovered she continued to fight for education rights.[28] At age 17 she won the Nobel Peace Prize, the youngest recipient yet. Now, she travels the world talking to others about how important education is. But, she always finds time for her own education.[29]

What if You Were Wrong about Everything?

Think about the last time you were wrong. Maybe you answered something wrong on a test or were trying to explain something when someone else corrected you. What does being wrong feel like? Embarrassing, right?

We bet not. The question was "What does being wrong feel like?" But when you're thinking about times you were wrong,

> "Then I'd be right about nothing."
> —Ben, Battle High School, age 17
>
> "Then what would happen if I said I was wrong about everything?"
> —Charlie, Battle High School, age 15

the feeling you remember arose just after you learned you were wrong. It can feel embarrassing to learn you are wrong, but actually *being wrong feels like being right* because you think you're right and don't yet know you're wrong.[30]

Being wrong happens all the time! If you thought about all the knowledge you have, you're probably wrong about a lot of it. You have a few beliefs that contradict each other, and you have beliefs about things in the world that will be changed by new scientific discoveries. You have beliefs that came about based on miscommunication or misunderstanding.

Now, what can you find that you're wrong about?

ACTIVITY
Comfortably Wrong

People usually aren't comfortable admitting when they're wrong. Why? They might think it makes them look silly or that people shouldn't believe or trust them. That's all pretty silly, though. What if admitting you're wrong is the first step in getting things right? The truth is, we've all been wrong before. What are some things you've been wrong about? What did you learn from realizing you were wrong? Journal three things you've been wrong about and what you learned from being wrong.

"If I was wrong about everything, I would stop answering questions and only ask them."
—Madi, Battle High School, age 15

"Nothing would change; the truth is subjective. My wrong truth is still my truth."
—Jonathan, Battle High School, age 17

What if You Wrote Computer Code?

Computer code, like any code, is made up of small parts that are like letters, words, sentences, and stories. Imagine you write a story, and your friend reads it. Well, that is kind of how computers work. A programmer writes out a series of events, descriptions, and comments in code. Then the computer reads the story and acts.

You can write recipes in code: start with peanut butter, jelly, and bread and then follow steps one, two, and three to make a sandwich. You can draw pictures in code: put the first box here and color it blue, put the second box three inches to the right of the first and color it red, and then put the first circle one inch above the second box and color it black.

Writing code allows you to easily manipulate how things interact with each other. If you had a robotic dog as a pet, you could teach it something (like how to guard your room) by uploading a bit of code to it. If you drew a house with code, you could change its size by editing the code (rather using a pencil to erase and redraw). If you built a house with code, you could change your room size, the color of your walls, and when the lights turn on—all by editing a few lines of code.

What would you change if you knew how to write code? What would you have your computer do that it doesn't do now? What would you make more interactive? A teddy bear that warms up when you hug it? Music that starts playing when you do chores? What would you want to make?

ACTIVITY
Write Some Code

Writing code doesn't have to be hard. It doesn't even require typing! Scratch is a programming language made by researchers at the Massachusetts Institute of Technology. With it, you can snap blocks of code together like Lego bricks. Go to scratch.mit.edu to put some blocks of code together. Maybe you'll draw something awesome, tell a story, or make the next Angry Birds!

ADA BYRON, COUNTESS OF LOVELACE, FOUNDER OF COMPUTING

Way back in the 1800s, Ada Byron met Charles Babbage.

From a very young age, Byron was interested in and inspired by the world around her. She tried to build wings for flying with[31] and, in her 20s, had an understanding of mathematics that surpassed that of men graduating college.[32] At this time, women were not encouraged to go to college or pursue anything intellectual. Ada Byron didn't care. She was going to learn anyway.

Babbage had been working on a Difference Engine, a mechanical calculator that could find answers to some complex mathematical functions. (Computers weren't around to do this because Byron and Babbage hadn't created their predecessors yet!) Imagine a large dining room table. Now imagine in the space the table takes up, from the floor to the ceiling, a contraption of gears, pulleys, and levers. That's what the Difference Engine looked like. When Babbage met Byron, he had a working prototype of this crazy machine and she was fascinated.

Some years passed before they started working together. Babbage lost his funding from the government and, at the same time, started work on an Analytical Engine.[33] This new invention would solve more than what the Difference Engine could—you could program it to solve new problems. They were designing a physical contraption that you program like a computer. Inspired by weaving looms that could make different patterns based on cards put in them, they set out to do the same with their mechanical computer.

Babbage saw the original potential, but Ada Byron saw an even bigger potential. What if they could use variables that could be filled with non-number symbols? She thought about having the machine manipulate language and musical notes, similar to how computers can edit sentences and write melodies.[34] The work was well before its time. Parts of the machine were built, but it mostly lived in sketches and notes, never completed.

What if There Was No You?

Where is the "you" in you? Some think it's your body. Some think it's your brain. Some think it's a combination of the two. Would you still be you if I took your brain and put it in a vat (where you could still think, of course!)?

Imagine a wooden ship called *Santa Maria*. After a year of being out to sea, it gets badly damaged. When it's back at the dock, workers find the damaged planks and replace them with new wood. The first time they fix it, there are many pieces to fix—50 percent of the ship. The next year the workers fix the ship again; this time they outfit 20 percent of the ship with new wood. The third year there is a really bad storm, and the workers have to replace 30 percent of the ship with new wood. When the *Santa Maria* sails for its fourth year, it doesn't have any of its original wood. It all got replaced by the workers. Is the *Santa Maria* still the *Santa Maria* that sailed out four years ago? If it isn't, where did the ship go? When did the change happen?

Here's the really weird part: your body and mind are like the *Santa Maria*. Every year, you have cells that die and get replaced by new cells. Every year, you learn new things and forget others. Do "you" exist through all of that? Do you constantly die, and then are you reborn? Is there no "you" at all? Are "you" the process of change—the shape of the river as water flows through?[35]

ACTIVITY
Talk with Your Friends

Ask around. See how people respond to the ship story and how they think about their own identities. Do they think they live and die all the time? Do they think they don't really exist? Do they think we're all processes of change? Or do they think something else? What do you think?

DAVID EAGLEMAN, NEUROSCIENTIST

Among other things, David Eagleman is interested in personal identity. Like the question above, he wonders where the you is inside your body. What makes it?

We like to think of memories, our personal life memory, as being at the core of our personal identity. It's what gives us a narrative of our lives that we can share with other people and has meaning to us. But the bad news is that it is not a faithful record. Instead, it is part of the ever-evolving story of who you are. [. . .] Who we are has so much to do with our experiences in the world. So, if you look across cultures in the world, you'll find that people and cultures and ideas are very, very different from one another, and this is because brains, human brains, are born into the world not finished. They drop into the world with the capacity to learn, and from there your experiences in the world tune up your brain circuitry on the fly. And so what that means is that so much of who you are has to do with your surroundings, your influences, the family [. . .] you were born into, your neighborhood, the culture you're born into . . . all of these are such an enormous part of personal identity.

We might have the fantasy that, let's say you were born one thousand years ago: what kind of person would you be? The fact is you wouldn't be you *at all*. You might look a bit like you, depending on the nutrition available, but internally you wouldn't be the same person at all, because, fundamentally, half of us is other people and our environment.[36]

What if You Became a Designer?

Design is about functionality, aesthetics, usability, and the small details. In other words, designers work to create systems that work really well, look great, and can be used by all sorts of people, and they're always sweating those little details.

Imagine some system or process. Maybe it's your morning routine, your computer, or even this book. Can you identify problem areas? What are the problems with the system or process, and what are some ways to fix it? That's the functionality part.

After you're done thinking about that, how does the system look? Is there a visual component? If there is, what looks great about it and what looks terrible? Thinking about this book, is there enough space around text blocks? If you only glanced at it, would you be able to pick out the important parts quickly? That's the aesthetics.

If your grandmother were using the system or process, would she understand it right away? What about your younger siblings? If you were color blind, broke your arm, or couldn't hear, would you still be able to use it well? Is there a large gap between how new users use the system and how people who've used it for a really long time use it? That's usability.

The little details are hard to find sometimes, but when you do, and when you realize why they are there, it makes you smile. Maybe the pockets of your pants are colored, but only on the inside. Maybe there's a menu that is only on the screen if you click on text that would use it. Maybe your hammer is designed to reduce vibrations when you're hitting nails. These details are subtle and can be hidden. Once you start examining your world every day, such details will start to pop out!

ACTIVITY
Improve Something and Prototype It

Look around you. What can you improve? Unless you're in the middle of an untouched forest, there's likely a part of your environment that was built by humans: a chair, a writing utensil, a photo, a sign, a building, a way to interact with something. (And even if you are in an untouched forest, you're likely wearing clothes, and you're definitely holding this book, so you're still able to participate in this activity.) Choose one of the things around you now. Pick it up (if you can). Examine it. What features can you pick out? Why do you think someone chose to make it that way?

Here's the fun part: What can you make better about it? Can you add or take away functionality? Can you make it look more pleasing? Can you make it easier for someone to use? Can you add a small detail that really gives the object or interaction character? Write and draw at least one thing in your journal for each category (function, aesthetics, usability, and small details).

CAROLYN DAVIDSON, DESIGNER OF SWOOSH

Graphic design is a part of the design profession that focuses on how things appear visually. These designers focus on typography, color choice, layout, visual patterns, understandability, and sometimes logos. In 1971, Carolyn Davidson was hired by Nike cofounder Phil Knight, at a rate of $2 per hour, to design a logo for his new company. She was a student at Portland State University at the time studying graphic design. She sketched a set of logos that needed to convey motion and look good on a shoe. The new company chose her sketch of a check mark, the now famous Nike Swoosh. When she finished her work, she made $35 off the logo. Though, in 1983, Nike gave Davidson 500 shares of stock.[37]

What if You Could Teleport Anywhere?

You're in a warehouse. It's big and empty except for a humming metal doorway in the middle of the room. As you walk up to it, you notice the space inside the doorway shimmers like light bouncing off water. You walk through it, and your shoe steps into . . . sand. Looking around, you realize the doorway brought you to a beach! You just teleported from point A to point B way faster than travel would have taken you in a car, plane, bullet train, or any other means of transportation known to humanity. Are teleportation machines possible? If you had one, how would you use it?

> "I would get more time to sleep in because I could factor out the time needed to travel. Patients could get to the hospital far faster than riding in an ambulance. Knowledge could be spread by simply walking through a teleportation device and arriving in a foreign place to share information. People could stay in touch with family that lives far away."
> —Madi, Battle High School, age 15

Teleportation is possible today . . . if you're a photon or atom.[38] Through complicated setups, physicists entangle particles to transfer the identity of one particle to another. Imagine if all you had to do to teleport was change your identity with someone else across the globe.

> "I would travel the world."
> —Kate, Battle High School, age 15

If we could teleport people or things across the world (or even across the universe!), how would society change? Right now, America is largely a car-based society. We probably wouldn't need all of those cars if we were just instantly popping in and out of places. What about war? We'd certainly have an easier time sneaking up on people, but we'd also be caught by surprise all the time too. Would we be less violent if everyone could just appear and disappear? And what about buildings? If we didn't have to walk through doorways, could we have huge buildings of closed spaces we just pop into?

ACTIVITY
One-Way Trip to Anywhere

The universe is a big place with many places to travel. It's easy to ask, "Where would you travel to?" Here's a harder question: if you had a transporter that could take you anywhere in the universe, but you could never come back home, where would you go? What would you need to find to be comfortable never coming back? Write your response in your journal.

"I'd get a spacesuit with a tank of oxygen and teleport to the moon just for fun. Then I'd travel across the world doing extraordinary things by teleporting things/people places in acts of trying to help them."
—Charlie, Battle High School, age 15

"I would never walk anywhere and wait until the last second for everything."
—John Ryan, Battle High School, age 15

What if You Started Your Own Business?

Businesses are all about solving problems. If you're in advertising, you try to figure out how to effectively sell a product or service to a market. If you're doing design work, you focus on functionality and usability for products or services. All businesses are the same in this regard. In business, you figure out how to deliver value to a customer (through products and services).

> "I would name it Stevo Candy. And make people happy."
> —Stephen, Findley Elementary, age 9
>
> "I would make it a snail farm, and snails would be a protected species."
> —Elise, Findley Elementary, age 10

Start by looking around for problems in the world. A problem could be something big: a country with a food shortage. A problem could be small: when people use a can opener made by XYZ Corp., they have a hard time opening their cans. This is where you come in. Find a solution to the problem. Figure out what works and what doesn't work.

Once you have a solution, try it out! The first answer is a step in the right direction, but it takes testing and refinement to make something really valuable. What do customers like and not like about your new product or service?

Sometime in the process you'll need to build a team. Who else can help you with this? What is missing in the current team, and how can you fill it with someone new? Teams take the load off one person and help you see things you couldn't have by yourself.

As you're making the next great thing, remember to check the market. What else is out there that might compete with you? What does that company do well, and what does it do poorly? How is your product or service better? If you offer something worse than what another company offers, can you make it better? Remember the big questions: Will people buy it? How much will they pay for it? Will you make money?

If you started a business, what kind of business would you start?

> "I would boss people around."
> —Noah, Findley Elementary, age 10

ACTIVITY
Seed an Idea Notebook

Spend a day with a pen and notepad. Every time someone complains about anything, write it down. Every time you think of something that could help someone out, write it down. By the end of the day, you'll probably have a lot written down! Now, skim through your notes and try to think of a few solutions for each problem. It could be something that already exists or something that doesn't yet. When you're done, do any of them catch your interest, and are you able to solve them? Could you sell the solution to people? If so, you might just have a business!

> "If I started my own business, I would make it unique, so it would not shut down—for example, a business that sold balls of water or floating cars."
> —Dillan, Columbia Elementary, age 11

> "I would sell pets, but I would only sell genetically modified squirrels that could do yoga, and I think it could be a hit."
> —Edward, Columbia Elementary, age 11

ALEX OSTERWALDER, BUSINESS MODEL GENERATOR

Alex Osterwalder has been challenging the way we make business models. After growing up in Switzerland and scraping his way through business school, he eventually wrote a book called *Business Model Generation*.[39] It explores business models in nine parts: customer segments, value propositions, channels, customer relationships, revenue streams, cost structure, key resources, key activities, and key partnerships.[40] Whoa. That's a lot. Let's break it down.

A business model is a bird's-eye view of how the business works. Customer segments are customers grouped by their similarities. When someone says "here's my product or service; it solves XYZ problem," he or she is giving you a value proposition. Channels are ways the business connects with customers (for example, social media, storefronts, and advertisements). Just like you have relationships with your friends, parents, and teachers, you can have a relationship with customers. That's customer relationships. Revenue streams are the ways in which you make money (your customers buying your products and services). Cost structure is all the ways you lose money (e.g., rent for your store and hiring people). Key resources are the objects you need to keep your business going while you're doing key activities (the activities you need to do to keep your business going). And, everyone needs friends. Key partnerships are the business's friends who also have important resources and do important activities.

> "It would be an encouraging business, so it can help you follow your true dreams."
> —Shannon, Findley Elementary, age 10 ½

> "Then I would make money by actually selling stuff instead of just getting an allowance for nothing."
> —Tanay, Findley Elementary, age 9 ½

> "I would own a mansion and live on a pile of money for a bed and own five thousand Teslas."
> —Olivia, Findley Elementary, age 10

An underlying theme of Alex Osterwalder's book, and of him as an interesting person, is focus on rapid testing. (A growing number of startup leaders focus on this.) When you're trying to make a business, you'll fail at something. It's his goal to help you both figure out why you failed and reconstruct your business so it can succeed. That's why he wants schools to help teach students how to fail successfully.[41]

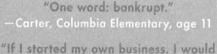

"One word: bankrupt."
—Carter, Columbia Elementary, age 11

"If I started my own business, I would start a business that would help the ocean. We would do beach cleanups, research about all different animals and plants, keep animals safe and wild, and teach others how to help save the ocean."
—Hilary, Columbia Elementary, age 11

"Well, I might, but right now when I'm ten? I don't think it'd work out very well. I could probably manage money all right, but getting people to buy stuff, I'd crack."
—Erin, Columbia Elementary, age 10

"It would be a store that sold smart talking rats as pets."
—Zephyr, Columbia Elementary, age 11

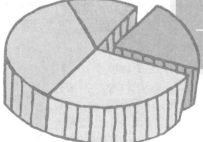

What if Your Parents Couldn't Tell You What Was Right and Wrong?

Imagine a world without any right or wrong—things just are. If people were loud in the library, they wouldn't be doing anything wrong. They would just be loud. People could run at swimming pools, eat all their food except their vegetables, and drive cars before they were old enough. Parents couldn't tell their kids to stop doing something because that something is wrong or bad.

What do you think this world would be like? Would it be crazy all the time? Or do you think people would still be nice to each other? Maybe people wouldn't yell in libraries because they would know that others go there for quietness. Maybe people would eat their vegetables because doing so gives them important nutrients. Maybe people wouldn't drive cars before they were of age because it is dangerous.

If there were no right or wrong, how would you act? Would you do anything you wanted? Would you be nice to strangers?

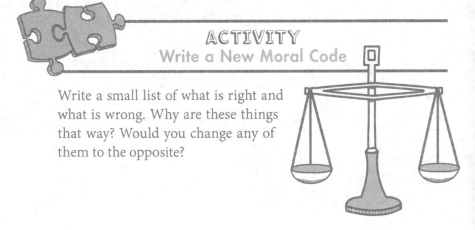

ACTIVITY
Write a New Moral Code

Write a small list of what is right and what is wrong. Why are these things that way? Would you change any of them to the opposite?

What if Society Were Truly Altruistic?

Altruism is the belief and action of acting selflessly. An altruistic act is one in which somebody puts another person first, even if it does not directly benefit the first person. In extreme cases, altruism may result in somebody making a personal sacrifice in order to help another person out. You can think of it as the opposite of selfishness.

> "I think there would be no war, and people wouldn't starve. I think our world would be much more peaceful."
> —Edward, Columbia Elementary, age 11
>
> "No one would be bullied."
> —Olivia, Columbia Elementary, age 10

Altruists believe their behavior can increase cooperation and improve harmony among all people. However, there are skeptics who believe that we, as individual beings, are always acting out of self-interest. For example, they might say the person who is "selflessly" helping others is only doing so because it makes that helper feel good or because he or she appreciates the thanks or recognition.

ACTIVITY
Secret Servant Agent

Become a secret servant agent for a day. Spend one day doing nice things for other people (for example, make your sibling's bed, do the dishes, rake your neighbor's leaves, write a letter telling someone how awesome he or she is, etc.) but do them without anyone seeing you or knowing it was you. Can you be stealthy enough not to get caught? If you can, how do you feel after doing these things that were kind to someone else but gave you nothing in return?

What if only you can determine whether altruism truly exists?

"I'm passionate about the various forms of oppression that plague the modern globalized world. If we worked for communal benefit, would stigmatism exist at all? Would all people be equal in this way? Would people of differing races, genders, orientations, and the like be equal?"
—Jonathan, Battle High School, age 17

"The world would be putting other things/people in front of something else. The world would be really nice."
—Cooper, Columbia Elementary, age 11

"Moms would be not awesome (which they are already)—they would be super awesome."
—Jake, Columbia Elementary, age 11

"There would be less articles about cyberbullying."
—Tashi, Findley Elementary, age 10

"They will not compete. There will also only be one society because they are all helping each other."
—Ervin, Findley Elementary, age 10

What if You Could Move Objects with Your Brain?

We already do move objects with our brains! Whenever you want to eat another bite of food, you have to reach out for it, pick it up, and put it in your mouth. Your brain has to tell your arm to move in such a way that you can eat. If it didn't, you'd probably starve!

But that's not entirely interesting, is it? So, what if you could move the things you can't move now with your brain? Lifting a car, moving a character in a video game, or playing your favorite instrument—what if you could do these things without touching anything?

> **"That would be AWESOME!"**
> —Jasper, Columbia Elementary, age 11
>
> **"We would be really lazy (no not really lazy—REALLY LAZY)! People will also have an advantage at robbing valuables. Then this power would be taken for granted."**
> —Aidan, Columbia Elementary, age 10

You can! Brain-computer interfaces, or BCI for short, are devices that connect the thoughts in your brain to the objects around you. Your brain has electrical signals in it. That's how thoughts move around and, in some ways, exist. These BCIs use small sensors that sit on your head to read and measure your thoughts.

But how does a BCI know the difference between your brain and your best friend's brain? Think about noses. We each have a nose, and each of our noses is unique. But there are a few properties that keep all noses similar: it's a pointy thing with two nostrils that comes out of a face. Brains are like that too. Each one is unique both in its structure and its thoughts, but

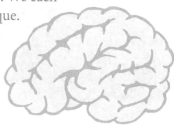

brains are also similar to each other. To help a BCI out, you have to train it a bit. You might do this by telling it you're thinking "up" when you're thinking up and "down" when you're thinking *down*. The BCI is looking for patterns of thoughts, and when it sees them, performs some action.

"I would wash the dishes without touching them."
—Stephen, Findley Elementary, age 9

"If we could move objects with our mind, then there would be no point in machines because you could make things make themselves. Also, people could stop asteroids from hitting the Earth, and people could change the weather by moving the clouds and sun."
—Emily, Findley Elementary, age 10

"The world would be destroyed by criminals."
—Elise, Findley Elementary, age 10

"Then people could move the Earth, and we could visit other solar systems and there would never be bad weather because we could move the clouds, and we would never have to build anything because you can make the materials build themselves."
—Francesca, Findley Elementary, age 10

"I would move my brain."
—Landon, Columbia Elementary, age 10

"I think I would be really lazy because I wouldn't get up to get things."
—Nevaeh, Columbia Elementary, age 11

"I would freak my brother out by moving something and telling him there was a ghost."
—Ceara, Findley Elementary, age 10

"I would win every time in darts, or soccer and other sports."
—Aiden, Columbia Elementary, age 11

After you train a BCI, you can do just about anything you set your mind to! (OK, that was a bad joke.) Brain-computer interfaces extend your mind and its capabilities. You could connect your brain to anything and control that thing with your mind . . . assuming you figured out how to find the

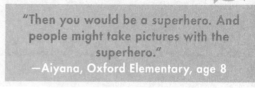

"Then you would be a superhero. And people might take pictures with the superhero."
—Aiyana, Oxford Elementary, age 8

patterns of thoughts and have a clear way of turning those into physical actions.

What if You Challenged the Rules?

Society has reasons for having rules, even if those reasons are not always very good. To become a rule, it has to be created, perhaps by people getting together and talking about why a rule is needed. A rule could come from one person in power deciding this is the way things should be. A rule could come out of a culture's practices. A lot of the time, rules can be pretty helpful. They tell you how you should act, and by everyone agreeing to them, you know what to expect.

For example, take the rule "don't steal." By people (or at least most people!) agreeing not to steal, you can feel a little safer when you walk down the street or when you pay for a product or make a trade with someone. If your fellow community members stole all the time, you wouldn't be able to trust them. And if you couldn't trust them, you'd have a hard time building organizations like businesses, schools, hospitals, and city governments.

The people who enforce the rules are generally called authorities. Your teacher is the authority on grades and homework. A police officer is the authority on speeding. Sometimes they only enforce the rules; other times they also create the rules. A parent is a good example of someone who is both the creator and the enforcer.

Now, how do we know rules are good? Well, if the rule stands up to tests and challenges, it's more likely a good rule than a bad rule. But if the rule gets questioned, and the authority can't give a good reason for why the rule is there, then maybe the rule isn't a very good rule to begin with.

For instance, in the United States, there used to be rules that people with darker skin couldn't be in the same places as people with lighter skin were. Blacks couldn't shop, eat, drink, or even go to the bathroom in the same places whites did those things. But people questioned this rule with a one-word question: "Why?" Is a difference in skin color a reason to separate people? Some authorities said yes, but many people kept questioning. Eventually, people realized that this segregation was a bad rule, and they changed both the rule and many of the authorities.

We live in a society with many rules, but not all of them are good ones. Which rules would you get rid of and why?

ACTIVITY
Challenge an Authority

The next time you get bothered by some rule an authority has, ask why the rule exists. If the person can't give good reasons, maybe the rule shouldn't exist. If the person can, maybe you'll learn something about your society. Remember: just because you're challenging something or someone, you can still be an empathetic person!

ALEXIS OHANIAN, REDDIT FOUNDER, ENTREPRENEUR

In his early twenties, Alexis Ohanian built Reddit, now one of the web's top fifty websites. He's challenged authorities by not always asking for permission before he acts. In his eyes, one of the great things about the internet is how much it empowers the people using it.

Every child who grows up with an internet connection and the skills to make the most of it is yet another potential founder, or artist, or activist, or philanthropist, or . . . I don't know, that's just it: I can look her in the eyes and tell her that she doesn't need to ask anyone's permission to go learn about the printing press, or start publishing her photography, or rally her community to fix a dilapidated playground, or begin working on the next big thing.[42]

What if You Kept Your Ideas to Yourself?

You are just lying in bed, about to fall asleep, when all of a sudden: BAM! POW! SHAZAM! You just had a good idea. No, not good—great. You have a great idea.

Where is your journal? Oh, there it is on the floor. You jot down the idea and go to sleep thinking about how many people will benefit from it (and how you'll make a lot of money in the process).

The sun rises and creeps through your window. It wakes you up. You blink a bit and then quickly jump out of bed to find your journal. There it is. Staring back at you are a few scribbles of brilliance.

What do you do now?

Through breakfast, on your way to school, and during class, all you can think about is your idea. You know it's really great. You want to tell people about it. But what if they steal it? They would get all the credit. They would go off to build the next big thing and be kings and queens of awesomesauce.

But maybe it wouldn't be so bad. It'd be cool to talk to your friends about it. Maybe they could help you. You could all work together to build something great. Or maybe they could share something with you that you would want to work on with them.

When you have that diamond of an idea, you might want to keep it to yourself. But here's the thing: ideas *want* to be shared. Ideas like to mingle with friends. Just like you

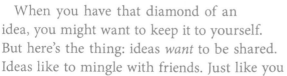

learn new things from your friends, ideas pick up new pieces too! Like you get smarter, ideas get stronger.

Most people can't execute their ideas all by themselves. Not because they are frightened to, but because those ideas need lots of hands to turn them into a reality. Many idea-building competitions require you to have a partner or team. Judges know teams work better than lone wolves.

So, what will you do the next time you have a great idea?

ACTIVITY
Build Your Dream Team

If you were about to launch an awesome new thing, who would join you? Make a list of your dream team. You can include your friends, other people you know, people you wish you knew, or even fictional people. Write each of their strengths (what they bring to the team) and what their weaknesses are. That way, you'll get an idea of how they might work together.

Part 3
Stuff

Stuff. The world is made of it. In fact, there are more inanimate objects on the planet than there are people. What would a book about curiosity be without some questions about all that stuff that makes our world?

Just because inanimate objects are, by definition, lifeless, it doesn't mean you can't find a life's worth of wonder wondering about these things we share our lives with. For example, your television, phone, computer, and tablet aren't alive, but could you imagine your life without them? Part of the reason that would be tough is because they connect your life to the lives of others. What if we need stuff to stay alive? But what if too much of some stuff could also lessen our living experiences? It's a tough balance, but what if, by questioning all the stuff in your life, you can get more out of it—and your life?

What if the questions in this chapter are also the silliest of the entire book? Questions like "what if broccoli tasted like chocolate?" and "what if your phone had feelings?" certainly sound funny, but what if there's also a ton of serious lessons to learn by asking silly questions about stuff?

What if Nanobots Joined the Fight against Cancer?

What if our biggest technological developments will happen on a very small scale? Nanobots, once just the subject of science-fiction stories, are about to become a reality.

Nano-whats? A nanobot is a tiny—and we mean tiny!—machine or robot that can work with other nanosize objects with precision. Just how tiny is a nanobot and other nanosize objects? They're anywhere from 0.1 to 1.0 micrometers in size.[1] To give you an idea how tiny a micrometer (or micron) is, there are 25,400 of them in an inch and just under a million of them in a yard (a meter has exactly one million microns in it).[2] If you pull out one of your hairs and stare at it, what you see is still about forty times wider than a single micron. A nanobot is so tiny, it could dig a hole through the diameter of a single hair and use it as a tube slide for fun.[3]

That is, if nanobots were designed to have fun. Currently, scientists are planning on giving the first nanobots they develop a lot of work to do. Considering that even red blood cells are over six times bigger than a micron[4], nanobots are ideal workers to help doctors treat patients and help humanity become healthier.

Today, cancer patients are treated with surgery or powerful drugs that can kill cancer cells, but they also damage healthy, noncancerous cells. This can be painful and as damaging as the cancer they're trying to treat. By injecting nanobots into a patient, doctors will be able to destroy only the cancer cells. Eventually, these nanobots could be designed to be scouts in addition to soldiers. What if your next visit to the doctor involved getting an injection of nanobots that would explore your body in search of diseases and eliminate them before they became deadly?[5]

OMID FAROKHZAD, PHYSICIAN SCIENTIST

Nanoparticles are small but powerful. Dr. Omid Farokhzad has created a few companies around different nanotech innovations he has helped pioneer. The nanoparticles in one of his projects do three things to attack cancer cells. First, the nanoparticle carries a cancer-fighting drug with it. Second, the nanoparticle's surface is water-like. That helps it sneak through someone's body without being detected and destroyed by an immune system. Third, the nanoparticle also has homing molecules that help it recognize and target cancer cells. When the nanoparticle collides with a cancer cell, it tricks the cell into letting it inside where the nanoparticle starts releasing its drugs.

Fighting cancer is a whole lot easier when you're fighting only the bad cells—and that's what you can do with these nanoparticles. There's a long way to go before average patients can start buying these targeted treatments, but research has grown exponentially. One day we'll take a pill that can help the immune system step up a notch and give us medicine right when and where we need it![6]

What if You Had a Box That Could Make Anything?

A box. That can make anything. *Anything.* Pretty cool, right?

Imagine there is a box in front of you. Maybe it is on a table. Maybe it is on the floor. Maybe it is just floating in the air. Imagine it as an entirely black box. There are no markings on the outside, but there is a lid. If this box could make anything tangible (meaning you can touch it), what would you have it make?

Would you have it make money, so you could buy things? Would you have it make a new friend to hang out with? Would you have it make you the tastiest food you have ever eaten?

These boxes already exist . . . kind of. The boxes are called 3D printers. These printers produce tangible objects. For instance, if you dropped your cup and it shattered, you could just print a new one. If you wanted a new part for your bicycle, you could just print it. If your friend came up with a really cool new toy, she could send the drawing to you and you could print it out! You see, all the information the box needs is digital, so it can move as easily as an email or text message. This works because someone draws up some object (like your cup or the new toy) on the computer. Then, the computer tells the printer how to print the object. That's it!

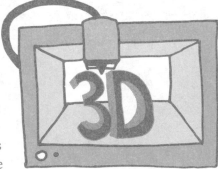

Right now, printers that most people have can only print plastic. But scientists, machinists, hobbyists, and tinkerers are working every day to make better and better printers that use other materials. Some of these are printing concrete—you could print a new house! Some are printing food—you could print that tastiest meal! Some are printing organs. Organs! What if one day you got into a car accident and needed a new lung? Right now you'd have to wait on a transplant list. But in the future, the hospital could just print you a new lung in a few hours.

Printers are coming a long way from just putting images on paper. Soon they'll print anything you can imagine.

TECHNICAL CORNER
How 3D Printing Works

Normal printers work by putting a layer of ink on paper. Instead of just one layer, 3D printers put many layers down to build up a shape. Look around you and find an object. Now, imagine you were to cut it into really, really, really thin slices. If you were printing that object with a 3D printer, it would print each slice/layer, one on top of the next, till the object was whole. They usually use plastic, but as you now know, 3D printers are starting to use all kinds of materials!

ALEX MADINGER, DESIGNER, INVENTOR, MECHANICAL ENGINEER

Alex Madinger has been interested in building things since he was young. In college, he was able to start playing with 3D printers, and he was hooked. Since then, he's been working on human prosthetics (artificial limbs). Often if you lose a limb, you'll get a generic prosthetic. But look at the people around you. Does everyone have the exact same arms and legs? Noooooope. So, wouldn't it be nice if there could be variety in prosthetics too?

Madinger's methods, like those of other 3D printing inventors, rely on a high level of customization and personal tuning. 3D printing methods allow inventors like Madinger to work more quickly because they can easily print and test their designs.

> If you have had an idea of something cool to make—and you've drawn it out on a piece of paper, you might not know [how it all works]. But you have a cool idea. Maybe someone has made it. Maybe someone is working on it. You can look online. [Either way,] instead of going to a big company to spend a lot of money to try to make your thing, you can use 3D printing.[7]

What if Your Phone Always Knew Where You Were?

What if you were never really alone? What if there was something—nonhuman—that always knew where you were?

If you have a cell phone, it's probably always close by you. Maybe it hangs out in your pocket or backpack. What if your phone knew where you were and knew where it was? What if everyone's phone was like that?

In some ways, this could be (and is!) really neat. You can have alerts that only come up based on your geolocation (*geo*—"world," *geolocation*—"world location"). If one of your favorite bands was playing a show in your town, your phone could say, "Hey! You! Go to this!" Or your local ice cream shop could offer a deal to whomever was within a few blocks of it.

In other ways, this can be (and is!) really terrible. Everything except for the physical laws that govern the universe can be hacked. That means a hacker, government, company, parent, brother, or sister could access your information and then know what you're doing and where you're doing it.

Here's a bonus "what if": what if your phone could predict where you go next? They don't call them "smart" phones for nothing. The more data our computers (and your phone is really more computer than phone now) collect about us—what we search, what we buy, what we watch, where we go, etc.—the better they're becoming at predicting what we'll do next.

> "First of all, [phones] already do. But because of this, it creates a major violation of our privacy because the fact that someone could always know where I'm at frankly terrifies me."
> —Dillon, Battle High School, age 16

"Wait. How does my phone know where I'm going to be? It doesn't have a brain." We hear you. You're right. Your phone doesn't have a brain, but it has something like a brain. It's able to collect data on you: what you like to do and when, where you go for different things, and with whom you hang out. Think about it. Every time you use your phone, you're giving it a little bit of information about what kind of person you are. Via data mining, it can look through all of those pieces of information, find patterns, and then make predictions based on your patterns. For instance, after noticing you driving to school at around the same time every day or going out to your favorite place to eat every Friday, your phone might start prompting you with the amount of time it will take to get to school or letting you know that that restaurant is getting crowded (because your phone is talking to other phones, which know what their owners are doing!). It's smart and a little frightening.

> "It better find me then when I lose it, stupid phone."
> —Ben, Battle High School, age 17

ACTIVITY
Map Your Location

Print out a map of your local area (make sure it includes where you are most of the time). For a week, mark your location on your map every hour with a dot and a number. The first place you are: a dot and a 1. The second: a dot and a 2. The third: a dot and a 3. You get the idea.

Keep doing this on and on (it's OK if you miss a few). After a week, you should have a map filled with dots and numbers. Place a piece of tracing paper over your map and connect the dots with straight lines. Don't worry about copying the dots or the numbers, just connect them on the tracing paper. When you're done, you'll have a new piece of art that is unique to you and your week.

If you want to go a little further, you could create other pieces of art based on your map. Or you could find a friend with this book, and you two could compare your location shapes.

AMBER CASE, CYBORG ANTHROPOLOGIST, FORMER DIRECTOR, ESRI R&D CENTER

Amber Case grew up excited about people and the technologies we use. She eventually focused her excitement on location-based technologies because they could tie information on the web to places in the real world. You could play games and leave messages for friends. Or you could help coordinate airplane flight plans and crowds at major events. You know, whichever was important to you.

There are all these planes out there, and trains, and ships, and people, and if they don't know where they are, they could be in serious trouble. So, a ship needs to know where it is in the ocean. Early location-based technology, like the compass, allows people to not sail into really rough seas, or get really lost and off track. It could help us explore new worlds. Now [location-based technology] makes sure your shipments arrive on time and that they aren't lost in a big storm.[8]

TECHNICAL CORNER
GPS

A global positioning system (GPS) is a collection of satellites and receiving devices that together help us find out where we are on Earth. It's important because it helps ships navigate open water, planes navigate the skies, and farm equipment steer itself, and it can also help you find your way in a busy city.

There are a handful of different ways to find your spot on Earth. GPS is one of those ways. Here's how it works: Your phone has a receiver in it that picks up signals from the GPS satellites. There are over twenty-five satellites that circle the Earth. They are all synchronized with each other, meaning they all have the same time on their internal clocks. Since it takes time for the signal to travel from space all the way down to your phone, and the satellites are in different places, each signal gets to your phone at a slightly different time. Your phone then calculates the differences between the signals and uses fancy mathematics to figure out where you are.[9]

What if Robots Looked Like People or Animals?

Think about a pet you know well. It runs around. It plays. It loves you. You've known it for a long time. What if one day you learned that this pet is actually a robot? How does this change your affection toward it? Would you love the animal just the same or be uncaring toward it because its brain is a computer?

What if you found out your best friend was a robot? How would that change your relationship with him or her? Would you still be kind? Or would you be more abrasive, as you might be to a phone, computer, or printer?

Robotics technology is very far along. Having developed faces that are almost human, and personalities that can be as complex as a kindergartner's, we're on the verge of more and more robots entering our lives.[10] In some ways, this is already happening, with Siri on iPhone and Google Now. Our devices are coming alive, and soon they'll have faces too.

There's a lot more we'll have to figure out in the coming years. If robots become as complex and mentally alive as humans, will they need rights similar to humans? If they need to get repaired at a repair shop, should they be able to get a license and drive themselves? If they are affected by government just like humans are, should robots be able to vote like we can? If a robot wants to run for a government office, should we let it? What if you developed a crush on a robot?! How do you think robots will change our future, and how will we change their future?

What if, instead of taking real animals from their homes in the wild, zoos used robotic, animatronic animals? How would you feel about going to a zoo of robotic animals rather than actual animals?

ACTIVITY
Surprise, I'm a Robot

One day your brother, sister, or good friend sits you down to tell you something serious, that he or she is not a human but a robot. How would you react?

Write a play or a screenplay (like a television show) that shows how you would react. You can choose whether or not you're a character in the play. Make sure to write some conversation, a few stage directions (where and when people should enter and exit the scene), and a description of the scene too.

SHERRY TURKLE, PhD AND ROBO-RELATIONSHIP CRITIC

Dr. Sherry Turkle studies the relationships between humans and computers (including robots). She has set up experiments and observations with both kids and adults playing with robots. According to Turkle and others, we have a tendency to want to be with robots, especially as they can fulfill our needs more and more. Humans are vulnerable. We're able to be hurt and able to be loved. If a robot can protect us from our fears of loneliness and of being hurt, we might just start wanting robotic relationships instead of messy human ones. And Turkle's research backs that up. She's found that we have a hard time distancing ourselves from robots when they give positive feedback (for instance, when robots light up and make cute beeping noises).[11]

What if You Had No Possessions?

If you could keep only ten things, of all your possessions, what would they be? What if you could keep only five things? Which would be your top three? What would be the one thing you would keep?

Nearly everywhere we look, there's another advertisement telling us the next great thing we "need" to make our lives better, easier, or both. But what if the secret to happiness was to reduce rather than reload? From architecture to fashion, artwork, design, and, now, lifestyle design, minimalism has been an attitude many have adopted. Is it even possible in today's consumer society? Would it work for you? It's tough to find out, because it requires a rather steep commitment (the first step is getting rid of all of your stuff!). What if you had to live with fewer things? Could you still be happy? Imagine going through an entire day with nothing other than the clothes you were wearing. Where would you go, what would you do, who would you see to fill your day and make you happy?

ACTIVITY
Your Top Ten Possessions

Choose a room in your house and imagine it is empty (or, if you're really adventurous, and with the permission of the adults you live with, actually empty it out). Choose only ten items to put in it. Take one away. How many can you take away before you lose your ability to use the room for its intended or required purpose?

"I wouldn't have a home."
—Luke, Columbia Elementary, age 11

"Then nobody would be greedy."
—Dillan, Columbia Elementary, age 11

"Then would I be alive?
I possess myself."
—Bailey, Columbia Elementary, age 11

"It would be weird if there were no possessions. We would have to measure with our fingers instead of a ruler, and we would have to use sticks as forks."
—Philippa, Oxford Elementary, age 9

"I wouldn't have to worry about losing anything because if I had no possessions I wouldn't care if I lost them."
—Kelly, Findley Elementary, age 10

What if Nanobots Turned the World into a Glob of Gray Goo?

Whether they're killing cancer or cleaning up pollution[12], nanobots are effective because of how they work together. Nanobots aren't lone wolves; they're a swarm. But just like any powerful technology, whether they're used for good or bad is, ultimately, up to humans to determine.

Just as a swarm of nanobots could be used to eat away harmful pollution molecules, they could also destroy the molecules that make up buildings—or you. There is a fear that swarms of nanobots could become the deadliest weapons of the future.[13]

There's also a fear of gray goo. Gray goo is the label for a scenario "in which a swarm of millions of rapidly self-replicating microscopic robots, in a ravenous quest for fuel, would consume the entire biosphere until nothing remained but an immense, sludge-like robotic mass."[14]

Take this scenario on how our world could turn from a lush planet of people, animals, and vegetation into a glob of goo:

> Take a relatively plausible present and future environmental problem/solution—cleaning a nature habitat after an oil spill. In this scenario, billions of nanobots are deployed to consume the toxic oil and convert it into less harmful substances. But a programming error directs the nanobots to devour all carbon-based objects, not just the oily hydrocarbons. These nanobots destroy everything, and in the process, replicate themselves. Within days—or hours—planet Earth is turned into "goo."[15]

What if Broccoli Tasted like Chocolate?

If broccoli tasted like chocolate, would we all be incredibly healthy or would we lose our appreciation for what it means to be healthy?

> "If broccoli tasted like chocolate, I would eat a lot."
> —Avery, Findley Elementary, age 10
>
> "It will make every kid eat healthy, right? And it will be ssssssooooo yummy."
> —Shannon, Findley Elementary, age 10 ½

Wondering about this raises a bigger question: Does this mean being and doing good isn't supposed to feel good, at least not initially? What if the better feelings we get are those we earn? For example, the feeling you get later on in life as a healthy individual from eating more broccoli than chocolate is certainly a better feeling than the quick flash of deliciousness on your tongue while munching on chocolate . . . right?

Sound farfetched? Consider this: What if there were a berry that, when eaten, would temporarily change how your taste buds taste? For example, after eating this berry, Tabasco sauce (that spicy hot sauce) would taste like doughnut glaze. Bitter things would taste temporarily sweet.[16]

ACTIVITY
Do the Yucky!

Make a quick list of ten things you hate doing—but know you should—like cleaning your room, doing your homework, being nice to your brother or sister, or eating your broccoli. Now, see how many of those things you can do today! Write them down once you're done.

How many did you do?

1–3: Come on! You can do better.

4–7: Not bad!

8–10: You just might be the most awesome person on the planet!

"I would have broccoli for dinner, lunch, and breakfast, and I would melt it and make green brownies."
—Vedant, Findley Elementary, age 9

"I would probably eat a lot more broccoli, but beans are vegetables, and cocoa beans are beans, and cocoa beans are used to make chocolate, so chocolate is a vegetable anyway."
—Schuyler, Columbia Elementary, age 11

"It would be horrible because broccoli tastes so much better than chocolate."
—Isaac, Oxford Elementary, age 9

TECHNICAL CORNER
Taste

On our tongues, we have different types of taste receptors. We know that there are at least five different types of receptors: sweet, sour, salty, bitter, and savory. Sweet receptors tell you that candy tastes sugary. Sour lets you know that's a lemon slice in your mouth and not an orange slice. Salty tells you that you've used too much of that seasoning on your eggs. Bitter is used for many things, but part of its importance is letting you know when foods have expired or are downright bad for you. Savory is part of meat's flavor, so you could also think about it as your tongue's bacon receptor. These five types of receptors are found all over the tongue, but the sides of your tongue are a bit more sensitive. All of these receptors work with your nose to let your brain know that the food you're eating is really tasty (or that you shouldn't eat it)![17]

"If broccoli tasted like chocolate, more children would like broccoli, but it would still be as healthy as it is now. Also, what would chocolate taste like?"
—Amy, Findley Elementary, age 9

"Everyone would eat it, we would have a broccoli shortage, and everyone would have to grow their own broccoli."
—Jeremy, Findley Elementary, age 10

"Then I would ask what does chocolate taste like, broccoli?"
—Tashi, Findley Elementary, age 10

"If broccoli tasted like chocolate, everybody would love broccoli. Every farmer would plant/eat chocolate broccoli seeds. It would be fun."
—Philippa, Oxford Elementary, age 9

What if Solipsism Were Correct?

What if the only reality was the one in your mind? That's the basic idea behind solipsism.[18] Since it's impossible to know what is in someone else's mind, a solipsist takes the perspective that his or her understanding of the world is the only one.

Sure, this might be seen as a very selfish and limited perspective, but how can you truly tell what is in someone else's mind? Or that anything is in their mind at all? What if

> "What if this was a dream? What if you woke up to find yourself in a different form? It would be a nightmare to wake up and what you thought was your life is gone, your family, your friends, everything is gone."
> —Hilary, Columbia Elementary, age 11

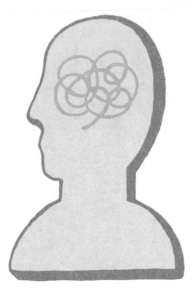

> "Then all your friends would be a dream? I refuse to believe that. If solipsism was correct, all the bad in the world would not even really exist—that would be good—but the flickers of goodness would be gone as well, not so good."
> —Erin, Columbia Elementary, age 11

everything you see and hear others do isn't them doing it; rather, it's just your brain telling you they're doing it?

Mind blown? Well, that's up to you.

"The Matrix, for realsies."
—Jake, Columbia Elementary, age 11

"I would take power over that and know that whatever happened was my imagination and do AWESOME things."
—Schuyler, Columbia Elementary, age 11

"We could actually be aliens in our teacher's mind."
—Olivia, Columbia Elementary, age 10

"If solipsism was correct, I would be in a constant fantasy. Who I thought was my best friend may be merely a tree. If solipsism was correct, the world may constantly be changing. We wouldn't be able to keep a stable leader, which would lead to a large amount of conflict. But it may help people be more creative and less worried about what other people think. But the most important thing to me is that people would feel unpopular or feel like they don't fit in. 'Cause to them they are awesome no matter what."
—Maximum, Columbia Elementary, age 11

What if Awesome Didn't Exist?

Does awesome exist? Do we create it? Is there any way we can control it?

Regardless, everyone seems to want as much awesome as we can get.

After all, a world without awesome isn't a world in which you'd want to live, right?

> "The word *awesome* is meaning to cause awe; if we didn't have wonder or awe, humans wouldn't be impressed with anything. The creativity of the world would decrease because they find nothing awesome enough to express ourselves with."
> —Kate, Battle High School, age 15

What if it were up to you to seek and create awesome wherever you are, wherever you go, and whatever you do, or it would disappear? Could you do it?

How would your life change? How would your community change? How would the world change if we created and shared the awesome we find all around us with others?

What if every day were an awesome day?

Believe it or not, for everyone who lived before the end of the sixteenth century, awesome didn't exist. At least, the English word for it didn't exist until around the 1590s.[19] And if people from way back then were to time travel to today, they'd

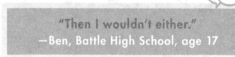

> "Then I wouldn't either."
> —Ben, Battle High School, age 17

discover the meaning of awesome has changed a bit with time. According to the *Online Etymology Dictionary*, the first definition of *awesome* was "profoundly reverential." Then, about eighty years later, its meaning was downgraded a bit to "inspiring awe." By 1961, *awesome* only meant "impressive, very good." What's up with that? It wasn't until the 1980s, though, that the word became trendy.[20]

What if you could determine the next definition for this awesome word? How would you define what's awesome?

HARVEY MILK: CIVIL, HUMAN, AND GAY RIGHTS ACTIVIST-POLITICIAN

Awesome means different things to different people. For Harvey Milk, awesome didn't exist yet. He wanted the gay community to gain a voice in politics. That would be awesome.

In the 1960s, Milk started to become more involved in politics, leading to his eventual appointment to San Francisco's Board of Permit Appeals. Harvey Milk was the first openly gay city commissioner in the United States.[21] In 1977, Milk was elected to the San Francisco City-County Supervisor position where he helped protect "gay rights [, . . .] establish day care centers for working mothers, the conversion of military facilities in the city to low-cost housing, reform of the tax code to attract industry to deserted warehouses and factories, and other issues."[22]

Harvey Milk and the mayor were assassinated by Dan White on November 27, 1978.

"Another word will replace its current meaning and the way it is used."
—Leslie, Battle High School, age 16

"I would invent it using my pet velociraptor and borrowing a knight's armor from a local museum."
—Charlie, Battle High School, age 15

"Then what would everything be?"
—Jonathan, Battle High School, age 17

That night thousands of supporters held a candlelight vigil in Milk's honor. "Milk Day" was created in 2009 as a California holiday in tribute to Harvey Milk.[23] He lived in a time with less acceptance of the gay community, and inspired others to come out, share their story, and shift public opinion.

What if You Could Get into a Machine That Created Any Experience You Wanted?

Imagine one day you get an offer from a mysterious stranger. She says that she can plug you into a machine that will create any experience you want. In the machine, you can do anything you can imagine. Your body will be taken care of by the machine. It will feed you and keep you alive, but while you are in it, you won't feel like you are hooked up. You'll be alone in the new virtual world but can choose to do anything. You could be president. You could be an explorer. You could live in a world where it rains every day. You would leave behind your family and friends. But you could always imagine a new family and new friends.

Would you want that? Would you miss your real family and friends? Would you get lonely with virtual friends? Would you feel like you are in a video game, or would you feel just the same as you do now? How would you change your world? What experiences would you want? If you would feel the same, how do you know you're not in a machine like this already? Would you ever leave the machine?[24]

ACTIVITY
Short Story

Write a short story in your journal about how you would respond to the mysterious stranger. Think about it before you start writing. Would you let her plug you in? What experiences would you want to have? Would you miss your family and friends?

TECHNICAL CORNER
Virtual Reality

Virtual reality (VR) is called *virtual* because it is an almost-real thing. These realities can be anything from a hyperrealistic world to an entirely made-up one that looks nothing like what you see every day. Video games are all virtual realities: a small set of objects that interact based on that particular universe's rules.

The really interesting realities are likely still to come. Over the last few years, a lot of traction has been put behind VR systems, starting with the development of the Oculus Rift. One of the problems is that VR systems can feel a little clunky. Your eyes are experiencing one thing while the rest of your body is just sitting still. It can be kind of like when you read in the car: part of you feels like it is moving, and the other part feels as though it isn't. Over time, we'll see even more sensory immersion with new interactive devices.

PALMER LUCKEY, OCULUS RIFT CREATOR

Humans throughout time have continually created imaginary worlds in their heads. If you're sitting around wondering what it might be like to fly a spaceship or be a doctor, you're imagining a fake world where you are that spaceship pilot or doctor. For almost as long as people have been using computers, they have also imagined and eventually even created simulated worlds they can "virtually" step into. Video games and 3D graphics were the beginning, but virtual reality (VR) was a goal.

Early virtual reality systems have been around since 1962.[25] This unique industry of creating virtual experiences grew like a balloon until, like balloons, it popped. The technology that the early innovators used was not good enough at tricking the brain into thinking it was indeed in a virtual world. And so excitement died down. VR headsets became the playthings of just a few research labs until one day 18-year-old Palmer Luckey created the first prototype of the Oculus Rift in 2011.[26]

Luckey was a curious kid. He did not understand why technology had not delivered more immersive, affordable experiences. So, he worked and saved his money, beginning to buy up the best virtual reality tech out there at the time. Still, the experience was lacking. Armed with curiosity, Luckey began building his own VR headset.

The Oculus Rift is a headset that you can wear. It has two screens and uses what is called stereographic images to put the wearer in a virtual world. *Stereo* is a stand-in for "two," *graphic* for "images." Two images are shown with a little distance between them. Each eye sees a separate image, and just like your eyes already work, your brain stitches the images together into a three-dimensional perspective of a virtual world. It wasn't the stereographic images that made the Rift exciting; it was that it created an experience so good, human brains had a hard time knowing they were in a virtual world.

Luckey's project started with a little curiosity. It continued with a dose of action—and money. Facebook eventually bought the company for $2 billion.[27] So don't let anyone tell you that questions aren't worth anything.

What if Everything Were Only Five Minutes Old?

You've been sitting and reading this book for more than five minutes. You remember eating breakfast this morning. You remember walking outside yesterday. You remember your birthday last year. How do you know all of that happened? Do you *really* know?

You've watched movies before, maybe even played video games. What if, somehow, you were connected to a machine that played a movie in your brain? Or what if that machine let you interact with things as though you were in a video game—all the while your body is sitting still (like the experience machine we what-iffed about earlier)?

What if, five minutes ago, you woke up out of nothingness but with all the memories of your life to that point? One way you could test if things existed before would be to ask someone if he or she had lived for more than five minutes. But what if everything—people, objects, ideas—all came into existence at the same time, but with memories of a longer past, only five minutes ago?

How is this scenario different from the Big Bang? What happened before the Big Bang? What if there was a whole universe that—all of a sudden—disappeared, and this universe took its place? What would be different in that scenario? How can you tell that the past exists beyond any point?[28]

ACTIVITY
Write Your Five Minutes

Find a timer and set it for five minutes. When it starts ticking, either write in your journal or record yourself speaking. Keep going until the timer runs out. Don't worry about being right or being wrong or being anything. Just keep going and going. A stream of consciousness is when you write or talk as fast as you think. There's no time to edit what you're writing or saying. Your consciousness is streaming out of your brain. (If you're embarrassed about anything when you're done, you can throw it away. But while the timer is going, don't think about editing.)

What if Everything Could Communicate?

Do you ever wish that when you woke up, your breakfast was ready, your shower was warm, and your favorite music was playing? What if everything were aware of everything else? Imagine that your house watched you wake up. If it knew when you woke up, it could start playing your favorite music. If you shower in the morning, it could prepare your shower by the time you walked from your bed into it. It could prepare your breakfast. And—the best part—it could save you time, so you didn't have to wake up a second before you needed to.

Imagine you get to school and your teacher doesn't have to take attendance, because the room knows you're there (maybe because of a chip in your phone, in your shoe, or in your body). After your teacher gave a new lesson, your desk or table could show you how that lesson is connected to other things you're interested in. For example, if your teacher was talking about mathematics, and you are really interested in whales, your desk or table could show how mathematicians calculate whale migration.

What would you connect? What would you never want connected?

ACTIVITY
Map the Connections

Look around the space you're in right now. Write down a handful of different objects that you see. Then, connect a few by drawing a line and writing about how they could be connected in the future. Your imagination is your limit!

What if Your Clothes Were Smarter?

When you buy clothes, what do you have to do? Try each piece on. Try different colors together. Try different styles. Basically, you have to test a bunch of different things to see what fits and what works well together.

People come in all different shapes, sizes, and styles. Why do our clothes have only a few available sizes? We have large, but not Susie-large or Bob-large. And everyone changes a bit even throughout one year. In summer, people may be more active and lose a few pounds. In winter, we're often less active and have many feasts—leading to us packing on a few pounds. These fluctuations are natural, but our clothes don't move with us.

What if our clothes were made out of new materials that worked with our lives better? Researchers are making clothing out of bacteria, allowing us to create more customized clothing with less waste (and possibly even have your clothes deliver nutrients to your skin!).[29] What if you didn't have to try on different colors and sizes? What if your clothes showed you where Wi-Fi was or knew your heart rate?[30] What if your clothes hardened when you bumped into something, which would protect you from accidents or punches?[31] What if your clothes got smarter?

ACTIVITY
Fashion Designer of Future Materials

Fashion designers of the future will have many more materials to choose from than we do today. But that doesn't mean we can't start thinking about new types of clothing in the present. Use the following inspiration list to design and draw new types of clothing you want to see in the future.

- Something that is made of plants
- Something that can talk to your phone or computer
- Something that can change colors
- Something that can change shape
- Something that can make noise
- Something that can broadcast signals
- Something that can receive signals
- Something that has multiple functions
- Something that changes when the weather changes

What if Your Phone Had Feelings?

What if your phone could understand and remember everything you spoke into or wrote on it?

If the lines between human and artificial intelligence are about to blur as never before, what does this mean for how we interact with machines? It's one thing to have your phone angry with you, but what if your computer-driven car hates your guts? Better look out!

> "If my phone had feelings, it would most likely complain all the time about me using it too much and repeatedly hitting the screen."
> —Veronica, Battle High School, age 17

Understanding how to read sentences or suggest restaurants you might like is one thing. But if your phone can read philosophical and legal documents, how long do you think it'll take before it wants to be able to vote and be respected like a human? How long will it take for your phone to want you to become a vegetarian because it cares for animals and doesn't want to see them on your plate?

What emotions, morals, and interactions will machines develop? Will they be in line with our own or something foreign?

> "I would apologize for all the times I yelled at it when I lost at a game."
> —Charlie, Battle High School, age 15

Could *machine* become its very own culture?

Or what if machines never develop feelings, yet how we treat them reinforces and reflects the way we treat other people?

What if it's time to tell your phone how much you appreciate him or her?

ACTIVITY
Create a Comic Strip

In your journal, make a comic strip about a phone with emotions (maybe even an emotional phone!). You can draw it or even cut images out of magazines. But try to make it funny, since comic strips are usually comedies.

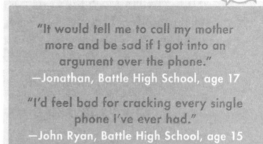

"It would tell me to call my mother more and be sad if I got into an argument over the phone."
—Jonathan, Battle High School, age 17

"I'd feel bad for cracking every single phone I've ever had."
—John Ryan, Battle High School, age 15

What if a Picture Were Worth
One Thousand Words?

You might have heard that expression before: a picture is worth one thousand words. But what does it mean?

Imagine you're telling your friend about a day you spent at the local museum. There, you saw this really great piece of digital art: an animation on a screen. If you're trying to describe the piece to your friend, how would you do it?

You first might try to tell him or her exactly what you saw. "Well, there was this line over here, and some shapes on this side, and colors all over the place." The more and more you talk, the closer you're getting to one thousand words. Maybe you skip a few details here and there, but if you do that, you won't be describing the whole picture.

Even after you've told all you can about the visual components of the art, there is still more to tell! Every human creation is sort of floating in a larger cultural story and the personal story of the artist. So, you might go on to say that the art you saw at the museum was part of an artistic movement. "During this time, artists from all around were using this technique," you might say, adding, "but this artist also included certain elements from her life." You're adding a lot of words, aren't you?

You could go on by sharing why the museum chose to add this piece to its collection, why you enjoyed the art, or even what other observers' responses were to it.

Or you could just show your friend a picture of the art.

ACTIVITY
One Thousand Words or Bust

Give yourself five minutes to find a picture. Put the picture up on a screen where you can see it or print it out. Now, get out your journal and start writing a description of the picture. How many words was it before your first long pause? Keep writing until you get to one thousand words (you might want to keep a running total of your word count every paragraph). Was it easy or hard to write that much about a single photo? What else did you learn about the experience?

What if Computers Were Conscious?

Computers follow a bunch of instructions. Turn on. Open the browser. Turn up the volume. They usually do what humans tell them to do. But what if they thought for themselves? What if computers were conscious like we are?

There are many stories about conscious computers and artificially intelligent machines (AI). Sometimes the computers take over the world because the humans are not needed anymore. Other times, the two live side by side. If we're living together with computers and they act similarly to humans, we'd need to change many of our systems. Would the computers go to school like we do? How would they be handled in court?

How would you know when computers become conscious? Would you measure it with medical equipment? How would you hook up the equipment? Would you ask the computer questions? How would you be able to tell if it was *really* thinking or just following a complex rule book?

Do you think computers ever will be conscious? What would they think about? How would you interact with one? Would it argue with you? Do you think its mind would be like yours or entirely different? What does it say about our minds if computers are able to think too? Should we treat computers differently just because their brains are different from ours? If computers can think, can they also feel emotion?

ACTIVITY
Watch a Science-Fiction Movie about AI

There are lots of science fiction movies about artificial intelligence (*WALL-E* is a fun one). Watch one and think about how AI is portrayed. Is the intelligence good or bad? How does it think? From the outside, would you be able to tell who is a robot and who is not?

TECHNICAL CORNER
Artificial Intelligence

There's been a lot of progress in creating smart machines that solve specific problems; we now have ones that produce Google's search results, win chess, and interpret our language in the way we speak. But so far, we haven't figured out exactly how to make a machine that can think as broadly as humans do. Computer scientists, philosophers, and engineers have a few different directions they are investigating.

One of those ways is by looking into our own brains. Since we know we think, the human brain would be a good model that we could break down and figure out how to reconstruct in a computer.

Another way is by having computers get better at symbol processing. You have thoughts, and your thoughts have symbols attached to them. For instance, when you're reading, you're looking at the letters and words on a page. You either know or are learning how to move those symbols around into other working symbols. You know that thinking is something you actively do, but a thought is an object. We might be able to make an AI just by strengthening its ability to manipulate symbols.[32]

Yet another way to build artificial intelligence would be to create a system or network of connections. Just like your brain has different sections that perform different functions, a network can do the same. For instance, if a computer is looking at a book and trying to figure out what the words say, it might have one small network looking at the shape of the letters, another network looking at the shape of the whole word, another one determining the meaning of one word, and yet another network determining the meaning of the words together. Each of these smaller networks can work together in a larger network to create an intelligence.[33] Which way is right? We don't quite know yet. All of them show some promise. It'll probably take some combination to create a truly thinking machine.

JOHN SEARLE, PHILOSOPHER

John Searle published a paper in 1980 that included the Chinese Room Argument.[34] This thought experiment has a man, who doesn't know Chinese, in a room with two slots in the wall. Through one slot arrive Chinese symbols. When they come in, the man looks up what to do with them in a very large book. The book doesn't tell him the meaning of the symbols, but it tells him what symbols to pass through the other slot.

Outside of the room is a woman who speaks Chinese. She writes down Chinese symbols and passes them through the first slot. Out of the second slot, she sees new symbols from the room. From her perspective, it seems like she's talking to another Chinese speaker. But from the man's perspective, he's just passing symbols out of the room based on what the book tells him to do. He never knows that the Chinese speaker is outside of the room nor does he even know that the symbols are Chinese. John Searle said that this is how computers work: based on certain inputs, they give certain outputs. Computers never understand what they are doing; therefore, artificial intelligence will never be truly intelligent.

This thought experiment is one of the most popular in philosophy and has sparked debate among philosophers, neuroscientists, and AI researchers. What do you think? Do you think Searle is right, or can you poke holes in his argument like others have?

What if Walls Could Talk?

We've been in many buildings in our lives: our house, our friends' houses, school, the doctor's office, the library, the grocery store. What if we could listen to what the walls have seen?

It's definitely a weird thought. If your friends saw you talking to a wall, they might think you need to see a doctor. Think about these buildings. They stand up to all sorts of weather. Snow, rain, hail, heat—all try to take a little piece out of the building. And what about inside? Workers come and go. If it's a family-run business, generation after generation fill the halls. If it's a school, the walls watch small children become young adults.

> "I would ask the wall what the answer to my homework is."
> —Stephen, Findley Elementary, age 9

What about major historical events? Older buildings have seen women enter the workforce, and racial desegregation. Think about how much technology has changed too! From paper and quill pens, to typewriters, to bulky computers, to laptops, to phones and tablets, to speech and gesture technologies—some buildings have seen this entire evolution. Some industrial buildings have turned into homes because the devices we use changed, in turn changing how we use our buildings.

> "They would tell us stuff they heard one thousand years ago."
> —Adrian, Oxford Elementary, age 8
>
> "That would be really scary."
> —Clare, Findley Elementary, age 9
>
> "If walls could talk, could they eat? If they could eat, what would they eat? Would they have mouths?"
> —Ceara, Findley Elementary, age 10

ACTIVITY
Listen to the Walls

Choose a building. Any building. It could be your house. It could be your school. It could be that one you look at every time you pass it. After you've chosen a building, start investigating it. Ask the people working there about its history. How long has the building been around? Who has used it and for what? Ask people in your community if they know anything about the building. You might also want to go to your city hall and look at the old building records. Write your notes in your journal. If walls could talk, you could learn a lot!

"I would ask the wall what it was like being a wall. Also, the walls would have to be living to talk, so you would have to feed the walls and give them water."
—Emily, Findley Elementary, age 10

"We would have more friends . . . and more enemies."
—Jeremy, Findley Elementary, age 10

"Then they would blabber all day about what it's like to be a wall."
—Tanay, Findley Elementary, age 9 ½

"When you ran into it, it would say, 'Oww!'"
—Nevaeh, Columbia Elementary, age 11

"Different walls would have different personalities, and they could tell you what colors they wanted to be, and what pictures or posters they would like, and it would be noisy!!"
—Calliope, Columbia Elementary, age 10

What if You Made Music?

BEEP BOOP.

Music can seem hard to make. Concert pianists, rock stars, jazz gods, and hip-hop heroes—they all can make great music, but they've worked for years and years to get where they are. How are you supposed to make sounds that awesome?

With a little pattern, that's how! Music is all about patterns— patterns repeated, patterns mixed and remixed, patterns adapted, patterns sped up and slowed down, patterns layered. While it's true that it can take a long time to create really great music, that doesn't mean you can't make something awesome right now.

Want to play drums? Start by tapping your hand on your desk. Tap it twice every second. Tap with an even space between each tap. Tap twice really quickly and then wait for the rest of the second. Now, try tapping twice every second with your right hand and once every second with your left hand. Try mixing up your taps. You're on the way to playing drums.

What about guitar? Try to find a rubber band or a piece of string. Take it and stretch it so that it's pretty tight. Now put your finger on it, pull it back a little, and release! Do you hear anything? Try tightening the rubber band some more (but make sure it doesn't break!). Does the sound get higher in pitch? What happens when you loosen it? If you play two notes, one high and one low, you've started playing guitar.

There you have it. You've started making music.

ACTIVITY
Really, Make Organized Noise

Music is basically organized noise. There's a noise over here, another over there, repeat. Anything can be an instrument as long as it makes a noise. You could use normal instruments, pots and pans, other noises stitched together, or even your own body to make music.

Your task? Make music in at least three different ways.

BILLIE HOLIDAY, JAZZ SINGER/SONGWRITER

Known for her low, coarse voice, Billie Holiday shaped jazz singing by performing her own works in a manner similar to how jazz is played: improvised and with changing speed. Her voice, coupled with her show of emotion, is what led Billie Holiday to popularity. One of her most notable works was "Strange Fruit," a song about the lynching of a black man in the south.[35]

Part 4
Nature

This section focuses more on the nonhuman aspects of nature, but it's important to remember our direct connection to the past, present, and future of nature.

We often think of nature as being everything that's outside and around us. That's true. But what if we're also a part of nature? What if we're not just a part of it, we also have a responsibility to it? Nature could survive without us better than we could without it. In fact, it did for billions of years before we decided to crash its party.

From space and time to plants and animals, nature is everywhere. What if questioning as much of nature as we can is the best way to make sure we can stay a part of it as long as we can?

Now, what if we got back to the questions?

What if People Could Sting with Their Fingers?

Sure, scorpions sting with their tails, and bees and wasps sting with their butts, but what if you had stingers in your fingers?

The stinging sensation you receive when you get stung by a bee or a wasp is partly from the stinger sticking in your

> **"LOL the fun I would have!"**
> —Ben, Battle High School, age 17

skin and partly from the poison it injects into you. So, if you've ever been stung by one of those critters, you can tell your friends you know what it's like to be poisoned. Scorpions, on the other hand, can control whether or not (and how much) poison they inject into you.[1] Who knows, if the scorpion likes you, it might not fill you with poison. Yeah, right!

A couple other animals you might want to model your stinger fingers after offer one of the world's most painful

> **"Could you then be poked to death then?"**
> —Charlie, Battle High School, age 15

stings, the bullet ant,[2] and one of the world's most deadly stingers, the box jellyfish.[3]

Incredibly, there is a man who studies stings—on himself! Justin Schmidt, a researcher at the Southwestern Biological Institute has been stung by over 150 of the world's most painful stingers. How does he describe the sting of a bullet ant? "They just make you want to lay [sic] down and die. You're just screaming in pain and agony."[4]

Scorpions use their stingers primarily for attacking animals they'd like to eat—but don't think you can bother one because you're too big to eat! Scorpions use their mighty sting to defend themselves too. Bees die after they sting[5], using their stingers to defend the rest of their colony.

How would you use your stinger fingers?

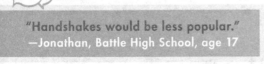

"Handshakes would be less popular."
—Jonathan, Battle High School, age 17

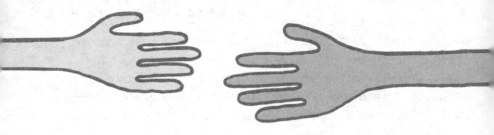

What if Time Repeated Itself?

What if, when you die, you are born again, and everything that happened to you the first time happened again . . . and again . . . and again . . . forever and ever on repeat? Think: every choice you made the first time around would be the same each and every time back through your life. If you did something wrong once, you'd do it wrong for infinity. If you were happy when you got your first pet, you'll be happy about it for infinity. You can't change any of your choices, but you do get to experience them again. It's like watching a movie on repeat but feeling the same things every time.

If you knew this was going to happen, how would you live differently? Would you live so each day brought you happiness? Would you live more selfishly? Would you live less selfishly, since you *and* everyone around you lives over and over again? If you were less selfish, the people you'd help would be helped for infinity.

But, from a different perspective, since you're doing the same thing forever, each time you do something, it matters less. Rather than thinking that this is the one and only time you can do something, you'd live as though each time didn't matter because you'd see it again for infinity. If you do something over and over, does it matter more because it will happen forever or matter less because it isn't unique?[6]

FRIEDRICH NIETZSCHE, PHILOSOPHER

In Friedrich Nietzsche's *The Gay Science*, he proposed a scenario in which life as we know it has already happened an infinite number of times before and will continue to happen exactly the same way an infinite number of times in the future. He used the story of a demon visiting one in one's sleep to examine how one might reconsider one's own existence—and the decisions made.

Below is the story of the demon Nietzsche used to explain this eternal recurrence, what he labeled "Eternal Return."

What, if some day or night a demon were to steal after you into your loneliest loneliness and say to you: "This life as you now live it and have lived it, you will have to live once more and innumerable times more; and there will be nothing new in it, but every pain and every joy and every thought and sigh and everything unutterably small or great in your life will have to return to you, all in the same succession and sequence—even this spider and this moonlight between the trees, and even this moment and I myself. The eternal hourglass of existence is turned upside down again and again, and you with it, speck of dust!" Would you not throw yourself down and gnash your teeth and curse the demon who spoke thus? Or have you once experienced a tremendous moment when you would have answered him: "You are a god and never have I heard anything more divine"? If this thought gained possession of you, it would change you as you are, or perhaps crush you.[7]

What if The Sun Never Went Down?

The Earth rotates on an axis (an imaginary line something turns on). You have learned that we travel around our sun. The Earth's rotation creates day and night. The day is the side of the Earth that is in sunlight. Night is the opposite side of the Earth where a shadow is created by the Earth itself.

So, "What if the sun never went down?" could also be asking, "What if the Earth stopped rotating?" (To be absolutely technical, it would be asking, "What if the Earth orbited the sun with the same side always facing the sun?") We'd end up being on a planet where almost half of the world would be in sunlight all the time. Almost another half would be in darkness all the time. The last little bit, the people on the border between light and dark, would live in a dim light similar to that of early morning or dusk.

> "Then what would happen to nocturnal animals? We would have more greenhouse gasses. People will never escape sunburns."
> —Aidan, Columbia Elementary, age 10

> "If the sun never went down, the plants would be green, nobody would sleep, and the California drought would be horrible, and I think the world would be a horrible place."
> —Olaf, Oxford Elementary, age 9

How would society change?

Think about farming. Plants need light to produce their own food. If there's no sunlight, plants couldn't grow, or we'd have to create artificial lights for the plants on the dark side of Earth. What about our sleep cycles? Your circadian rhythm is your "around day" rhythm. It's what your body goes through every day. When you get tired late at night, it's because certain hormones start to run through your body. Around 2:00 AM is your deepest sleeping time. You become alert throughout the day. Your daily rhythm changes a bit with the environment around you. You become more alert if your body knows the sun is up (and more tired when it drops and it gets dark). Think about whole societies in which the rhythm is thrown off. We'd have to set up light areas on the dark side and dark areas on the light side.

"There would be no night, and we would never see the stars or moon, and since the stars are so far away, we would never know about them, and there would not be the song 'Twinkle, Twinkle, Little Star.'"
—Francesca, Findley Elementary, age 10

How do you think we'd have to change? What else would we need to fix? What would get better if we did this?

ACTIVITY
Stay Up All Night

Ask your parents to let you stay up all night. Tell them it's OK—this book says so. Journal your experience every hour. What do you do with your time awake? How tired do you get? Do you get bored? Is it lonely when you're the only person up? Did you make it through the night?

"I would play soccer late at night."
—Edward, Columbia Elementary, age 11

"One part of the world would freeze."
—Zephyr, Columbia Elementary, age 11

"I would stay up as long as I could and play all day every day."
—Conner, Columbia Elementary, age 11

What if There Weren't Any Trees?

No trees? That's a terrifying thought! Where would birds sing? Where would squirrels play? What would kids climb? Where would you go for shade when the sun is blazing?

> "Humanity would focus on algae farms in order to create an adequate oxygen supply."
> —Jonathan, Battle High School, age 17

This scenario might not be that hard to imagine. All it takes is a quick look at pictures from one of the many deserts on earth to get an idea of what a treeless spot would look like. You could also look at photos from Mars to get an idea of what an entire planet without trees would look like. Looks kind of boring, huh?

Aside from the things we see and do with trees, did you know they serve several other functions you don't see? For example, trees make it easier for us to breathe. Not only do they breathe in carbon dioxide (what we breathe out) but they breathe out oxygen. That's right, trees use what we don't need and give us back what we need. No offense to dogs, but what if trees are humans' best friend? But that's not all—their roots, deep underground, help prevent erosion and keep ecosystems strong. Even though

> "There would be no living life on Earth due to each animal and species needing air to survive."
> —Leslie, Battle High School, age 16
>
> "Then the birds would be living in caves."
> —John Ryan, Battle High School, age 15

trees don't move a lot, they're extremely active in keeping the other living things on this planet healthy.

What kinds of things could you do to make sure our planet never runs out of trees?

ACTIVITY
Plant a Tree

Here's a first step to making sure we never run out of trees: plant a tree. Depending on the time of year, you could find a seed off an existing tree. If you like oaks, look for those acorns! If you can't find any seeds, you could go to an arboretum or a plant nursery and buy one. Around Arbor Day, the last Friday in April in the United States, you can usually find some trees for free. Plant one and breathe a little easier.

JOYCE KILMER, POET

What if the pen is mightier than the sword? Or the poem is mightier than the chainsaw?

Poet Joyce Kilmer's famous poem "Trees" opens with the lines: "I think that I shall never see / A poem lovely as a tree."[8]

Three years after "Trees" was published in 1914, Kilmer enlisted to fight in the First World War. Tragically, during the battle of Ourcq, on July 30, 1918, Kilmer was cut down by a sniper's bullet.[9]

After Kilmer's death, "Trees" became even more popular among American readers. The poem and its poet became so popular that, in 1938, the US government went as far as to purchase thirty-eight hundred acres of forest in North Carolina, dedicate the land to Kilmer's memory, and stop extensive logging in the area. Today, the Joyce Kilmer Memorial Forest is one of the best examples of old-growth forests in the United States, with over one hundred different species of trees, many of which reach one hundred feet tall and twenty feet around and have been around for over four hundred years.[10]

> "Earth would look like Mars, and we would be dead."
> —Charlie, Battle High School, age 15

What if People Got Energy from the Sun?

Every day, we humans have to eat. Getting food into our stomachs is a *huge* process. The sun has to shine on plants. The plants have to use a process called photosynthesis to convert sunlight into sugars they can eat. (*Photo* relates to light, and *synthesis* means "bring together to make something new.") Animals eat some of these plants. Then farmers harvest, wash, and take the plants to the store. Farmers butcher animals and take them to the store too. People buy food from the store, take it home, and then prepare it. All of this happens before we take one bite. But what if we got our energy from the sun just like plants do?

> "People wouldn't have to spend time worrying about their next meal, acquiring food, or even sitting down to eat food. Also, this function would limit where humans could live. Areas that receive less sunlight than others would be dangerous places to live."
> —Madi, Battle High School, age 15

We would just have to go outside to "eat." If you got hungry late at night, maybe you would go to the new fast food restaurant: a tanning salon. We'd probably add more windows to our buildings, so we could be full all the time.

If we only ate through photosynthesis instead of through our mouths, what else would change? Farmers would grow only decorative plants or work on biofuels (fuel made from plants). Grocery stores wouldn't exist anymore. In the transition from normal food to sunlight, we'd have so much livestock that wouldn't be eaten. What else do you think would change?

ACTIVITY
Write a News Story

Journalists are the people who write news stories. Now it's your turn to be a journalist. Write a short news story that is introducing a new species of human that can use photosynthesis. Maybe there was a government lab experiment? Maybe a group of individuals tested new drugs on themselves? Maybe someone just woke up one day and didn't have to eat if

"We would be like plants. I would be very sad because I love food and enjoy eating."
—Kate, Battle High School, age 15

he or she sat in the sun? We don't know. But we will after you write your story.

TECHNICAL CORNER
Photosynthesis

Plants turn sunlight into energy all the time. Photosynthesis is a very complicated and involved process. We bet it's harder than the next test you'll take.

In its simplest form, photosynthesis is the process plants use to convert sunlight into usable energy. Light from the sun hits the surface of plants and gets absorbed by chlorophyll. The chlorophyll gets excited with its new energy. Through a series of chemical reactions, that energy then gets converted into sugars plants can use to grow. During the process, plants consume carbon dioxide from the air (what you breathe out) and output oxygen (what you breathe in). So, when plants are making their food, we get more stuff to breathe![1]

"World hunger would thankfully be gone; water scarcity would be even more important as it would still be required for photosynthesis."
—Jonathan, Battle High School, age 17

"I would have no energy. I do not like the sun. It would be a two-edge sword. You get large amounts of energy, and skin cancer."
—Charlie, Battle High School, age 15

Recipe
Ingredients
sun, sun, sun, sun, and more sun

What if Humans Had Elephant Noses?

If you had an elephant nose, what would you do with it: pick things up or spray water?

If you said pick things up, you might be surprised at just how many things you'd be able to grab with your trunk. Elephants can grab things as tiny as a marble and larger than a basketball.[12]

> "I'd spray people with water more often."
> —Charlie, Battle High School, age 15

If you said spray water from it, you're probably already imagining your brother or sister as a target. But you might also want to consider using this powerful sprayer for defense—a very dusty defense.

Did you know an elephant's nose isn't used to spray only water? Elephants use their trunks to spray dust as well. Why? Coating their bodies in layers of dust protects elephants from both the sun's rays and insect bites.[13]

> "Slapping people would be a lot more fun."
> —Andrew, Battle High School, age 15

Grabbing and spraying things are just the beginning of how you might use an elephant trunk if you had one for a nose. Elephants also use them to dig holes in the ground, and they show affection by caressing each other with them.

That's a whole lot of work, considering all your nose right now does is smell and collect boogers. What crazy things would you put your elephant nose up to if you had one?

ACTIVITY
Build Your New Nose

Find some cardboard and build yourself a new nose. Cardboard is an extremely versatile material. It can be cut into shapes, glued together into structures, and even be folded into a chair that can hold you up (do an image search to find some really awesome cardboard chairs). You could create a long elephant nose, a short pig nose, or a wild nose no one has seen before. Go ahead and use other materials like glue, string, and paint, if you'd like. Make sure to put a picture of yourself wearing your nose in your journal.

What if You Could See the Color of Nine?

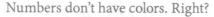

Numbers don't have colors. Right?

Some people's brains have a condition called synesthesia. For them, senses can get crossed. Some people with synesthesia see the colors of numbers. For instance, when they see the number nine, it might always be green. Three could always be light blue. Four could always be deep yellow. Math would be pretty different if you could see how numbers relate by seeing their colors interact!

Some people can hear colors. Orange might be a trombone playing a quick chirp. Violet might be a violin humming back and forth. Going to an art museum would be like going to a concert hall with a full orchestra!

> "I would cross my sense of taste with my sense of hearing, so I could taste ice cream when someone said 'ice cream,' and I could taste screams, and if they tasted good, I would know it was happy and if it tasted bad it would be sad."
> —Schuyler, Columbia Elementary, age 11

"Yellow, with accents of mustard and sherbet orange."[14] That's the color of the hit song, "Happy," according to its artist, Pharrell Williams. Synesthesia can take over seventy different forms, such as tasting or smelling sounds, but the most common is hearing colors. Williams is part of the 4 percent of the population who have synesthesia. While synesthesia is rare among the general public, it's quite common among artists. Kanye West, Frank Ocean, and Lady Gaga are synesthetes who can hear colors, just like Vincent van Gogh, Duke Ellington, and Marilyn Monroe did before them.[15]

> "Then you could see the color of 1, 2, 3, 4, 5, 6, 7, 8, 9, 10 . . . and in math you could say 3 x 3 = yellow."
> —Vedant, Findley Elementary, age 9

If you could cross your senses, which would you cross?

ACTIVITY
Your New Senses

Seeing the color of nine or hearing red would be pretty strange for the majority of people, who have never done such a thing. For this activity, think of a few ways you could pick up a new sense. What could you do by blending sound, color, motion, taste, and touch? Write up your thoughts in your journal.

NEIL HARBISSON, SYNESTHESIA CYBORG

Neil Harbisson was born with a syndrome called achromatopsia, meaning total color blindness. His whole world is different shades of gray. However, when he was in his early twenties, Harbisson started working with a computer scientist to change the way Harbisson perceives color. They made a third "eye" for Harbisson and attached it to his skull. The new eye sees a color, which transmits a signal to his skull, which vibrates his skull, which allows him to hear that color. Although he can't see colors

> "I would freak out."
> —Nestor, Oxford Elementary, age 9

with his eyes, Harbisson can at least hear the patterns we see with our eyes. What if you could hear what your banana's color sounded like? That's what Harbisson wondered. When he goes to the grocery store or an art gallery, Harbisson hears symphonies of sound. Both weird and awesome, right?[16]

"If I could see the color nine, than I bet it would be a tiger pattern with black and blue."
—Winnie, Oxford Elementary, age 9

"I think it would be yellow, because yellow is mellow. Nine is mellow."
—Nevaeh, Columbia Elementary, age 11

"That would be colorful! I would like that a lot. People might see different colors, or they might all see the same color."
—Calliope, Columbia Elementary, age 10

"Then I would be jealous of the people who can see the color of ten."
—Tashi, Findley Elementary, age 10

What if Humans Had See-Through Bodies?

A see-through body? Sounds pretty crazy . . . and really, really gross. Even if you had a see-through body, you wouldn't be the first animal to be transparent. Many animals in the deepest reaches of the oceans have see-through bodies. They do so because, with such little light in the depths of the ocean, being transparent makes them very difficult to see. Being see-through becomes their most effective camouflage against their predators.[17] When you consider there aren't a lot of rocks, bushes, trees, or other objects to hide behind, being able to hide in plain sight is incredibly important in the deep ocean.

> "When I ate food, would I see it digesting, or would it just disappear?"
> —Charlie, Battle High School, age 15

Not only are there already animals with see-through bodies, but scientists apparently don't believe there are enough. Some scientists are now working to create see-through mice.[18] But these aren't mad scientists. They're not making mice transparent as part of some sick and twisted experiment. Instead, they're doing it to better understand the inner workings of living things. Being able to watch bodily functions (such as digestion) as they take place could help scientists make new discoveries that might help us all live healthier lives.

If you could watch how your body reacts to and processes the different foods and drinks you put in your body, would it change what and the way you eat? If you could see how your organs performed after a good night's sleep—and after staying up late—do you think you'd change the way you sleep?

What would you do with your see-through body? Would you use it for camouflage, to gross out your friends, to learn more about your body, or something else?

ACTIVITY
Video Voice-Over

Have you ever heard a funny voice-over, or dub? That's when one video is playing, but a different audio track is playing simultaneously. Some movies use dubbed voices when the actors speak a different language than the audience speaks. Animated movies have to do this too. Those drawn or computer-generated characters aren't real people who speak, so the actors record their voices and put them over the visuals.

Find a video or record one. Then, record your voice over the visuals. You have to speak about something related to humans having see-through bodies. You could make up a conversation between two people or do a documentary-style narration. You can write out different scripts in your journal.

"Medicine would be a lot more advanced."
—Andrew, Battle High School, age 15

What if Humans Had Skin That Changed with Their Surroundings?

If you could change your skin so it matched your surroundings, you'd be invisible. Pretty cool. But what if cool powers come with heavy responsibilities? Would you use your ability to blend in with whatever was around you to protect yourself from danger? Would you use it to become a world champion hide-and-seek player? Or would you use it to spy on people when they didn't know you were there?

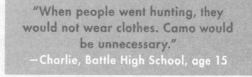

> "When people went hunting, they would not wear clothes. Camo would be unnecessary."
> —Charlie, Battle High School, age 15

This is an age-old question brought up by the philosopher Plato in his book *The Republic*. Plato told the story of the Ring of Gyges (a story about Gyges, who finds a ring that makes him invisible) and asked people what they would do if they had Gyges's ring. After listening to their answers, Plato could gauge how decent each person was.[19]

While Gyges's invisibility is fictional, there are real animals that can really change their skin according to their surroundings. Perhaps the most well-known is the chameleon. But did you know octopuses are expert skin-changers too? The mimic octopus, for example, doesn't

> "I'd skip class all the time."
> —John Ryan, Battle High School, age 15

change its skin color to match its surroundings—it changes its skin to look like other sea creatures'. It's been able to learn how to look like fifteen different underwater animals, such as seahorses, sea snakes, and flounders.[20]

What if You Could Give Your Pet a New Ability?

Ever wish your fish could glow in the dark or your dog could smell like roses? Which abilities would you give to which pets? Invisibility? Wings? Maybe make their own food from the sun so you don't have to feed them?

The cells in our bodies have something called DNA. DNA is made up of a sort of code, a type of chemical description for our physical features. Have curly hair? It's because your DNA tells your hair to grow in curls. If you were to change a bit of your DNA, you could change how curly your hair is, how tall you could grow, or even, to some degree, how long you could run. Your pets have DNA too. Change a bit of their descriptions, and they could have new abilities.

This is where things get really interesting. If you were able to find out how to put a piece of glowworm DNA into your fish, you could use your fish as a nightlight. If you could give your dog the right bit of fish DNA, your dog could grow gills and breathe underwater.

Researchers are exploring ways to change DNA right now! They're trying to make trees grow certain ways.[21] Imagine a seed that would grow into a bookcase! They're also modifying algae DNA so that the modified algae produce fuel for cars.[22] Rather than digging fuels out of the ground, you could just grow some at your house. Think of all the possibilities!

Would you want to change your pet? Is it right to change your pet's abilities? Is it possible to love something for what it is *and* want to change it?

ACTIVITY
Draw Your New Pet

Draw a pet with new abilities! Would you want a cat with wings? A pocket-size whale? A pink zebra? What would your new pet look like, and what would it be able to do?

TECHNICAL CORNER
Synthetic Biology

In a few short years, you'll probably be able to create your own creatures by stitching pieces of DNA together. This would work similarly to how you might create a new story by cutting and pasting pieces of other stories together. College students are already creating newish creatures in a competition called iGEM. They use, like you might one day, Bioblocks: a toolbox of genetic material. If you want your little bacterium to have a tail that spins, you just select that set of genes and have a machine stitch it together.

The field of creating new organisms and creating old organisms with new genes is called synthetic biology. It's not science fiction. It's real.[23]

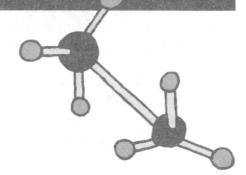

What if Ants Solved Problems Every Day?

Have you ever sat and watched ants? At first they seem to scurry around every which way. Do they know what they're doing? Look closer! Those ants are solving problems.

Ants need food like we do. When ants leave the colony, they do wander without direction. Each ant has no idea what is going on. As it turns out, most ants can't see very well, but they are expert smellers.[24] As they walk, ants lay little pheromone markers down— it's a smell trail other ants can pick up on.[25] If an ant finds food, it grabs some and walks back to the colony. Now, imagine this happening again and again. Soon there would be really strong smell trails where the ants found food and found short paths to it. There would also be weak smell trails where ants got lost or took a really long path. As the next ant leaves the colony, it wonders which way to go. Because of the smell paths, it can choose the strong one to go find food quickly. Thanks, ants! Or, *thants!*[26]

But that's not all they can do. Ants build massive underground networks to live in. When trying to cross a gap, some ants build a bridge *out of other ants*. A few of them just hold on to the sides and to each other while their ant friends walk over them. There are even ants that, when dropped in water, cling together to make an ant raft. You can try to sink them, but they hold tight.[27]

Even though ants might steal food from your picnic, they do so efficiently—they are pretty good at finding the shortest path to your food! One ant can't figure out the best way. But when ants work together, they solve problems every day.

ACTIVITY
Do It the Ant Way

This one is a little messy.

First, find a few friends to play with you. Then, take paper and tear it up into tiny pieces, like breadcrumbs, and give some pieces to everyone. Next, choose somewhere in your house that will be your "anthill," your home base. (Maybe the kitchen, so you can enjoy a treat after this crazy game!) You and your friends now make trails to interesting places in your house. Each of you should start by going in a direction different from the others. As you walk, drop a trail of paper behind you. After you find somewhere interesting, walk back (following your trail) to your anthill. Now, follow one of your friend's tracks to the place that person found interesting (make sure to drop your own trail down too).

Keep doing this until you find the most interesting place. Once you find it, keep going back and forth along your chosen trail to see if your friends agree. If you all end up on the same path, you've found the most interesting place in your house. If you've been walking for a while and just can't agree, call a time out and grab a snack. There must be more than one interesting place in your house.

What if There Were No Luck?

Luck is tough to prove. If you could be convinced that there is absolutely no such thing as luck, what would be the first thing you'd start doing differently?

Are we too swayed by luck? If there were no luck (good or bad) and therefore no chance luck could affect anything you do, how might that change the way you live? What if how well you did on your next test, performance, or game depended on you and only you? How would this change the way—and the amount of time—you prepare for the things you do? How would this affect your future failures . . . and successes?

But what if there were a few things you could do to make you and your life at least *seem* a lot luckier? Believe it or not, people actually study luck. While their studies show luck does not exist, they have uncovered certain behaviors of people who believe they are lucky. Want to create your own luck? Follow these steps:

1. Be open to new ideas and unafraid of change.
2. Expect the unexpected. Often, what we confuse with luck is just unexpected fortune.
3. Hang out with many different people, including people from different backgrounds. Different people in our lives often deliver good news and great opportunities.
4. Break out of routines. Doing the same thing the same way keeps things the same. If you're feeling unlucky, why would you want that?

5. Be optimistic. Learn to turn negatives into positives; while it won't make you lucky, it will reduce the number of negatives in your life.

6. Expect to be lucky! What do you have to lose?

ACTIVITY
Create Your Own Superstition

Many people develop superstitions when they start believing luck is a result of routine. Create your own superstition by establishing a ritual, or routine, that you do every day. Below, make a list of the actions, words, and time of day your ritual must be done in order to bring good luck. Make it silly, fun, and useful by choosing actions that prepare you for a happy and focused day. See how many other people you can convince to take it up.

What if You Could Travel at Almost the Speed of Light?

Light travels super fast. Really super fast. If nothing is in its way, the speed of light is about 670,600,000 miles per hour! See? Really fast. The speed of light is kind of like a big universal speed limit. It's not like the speed limits on the highway, where you can still go faster. It is the fastest speed at which something can travel in the universe.

> "You would never age because you would be going so fast."
> —Mason, Columbia Elementary, age 11

When objects travel really fast, weird things happen. As you accelerate toward the speed of light, time dilates. What that means is that it kind of stretches out.

You decide to build a rocket to get you to almost the speed of light with your friend, who is the same age as you. Luckily, you get to ride the rocket while your friend has to stay on Earth. After your launch, you're zipping through space at 99 percent of the speed of light! You can't see well out of your ship because things are moving too quickly past you. After a year, you've had enough space travel and decide to head back to Earth (taking another year).

> "Then I would become part of the FBI or the army because it would be easy to dodge attacks/bullets, and I would be world famous."
> —Schuyler, Columbia Elementary, age 11

> "I would never be late for school."
> —Jake, Columbia Elementary, age 11

When you land, your friend greets you *but is fourteen years older*! Time dilated for you because you were traveling so fast. While your friend was aging normally, you were aging slowly because of how fast you were going!

TECHNICAL CORNER
Light Speed, and No Faster

Why can't we go faster than the speed of light? If you're in a car going twenty miles per hour, the driver can pretty easily speed up to sixty miles per hour. Why can't we just keep speeding up to the speed of light and beyond?

Like we learned in the question, time dilates. It expands. That means your personal clock ticks slower the faster you're moving. If you were to hit the speed of light, time would stop for you.

As you speed up, it also takes more and more energy for every additional mile per hour. To actually reach the speed of light, you would need infinite energy. Since you can't get infinite energy, you can't move at the speed of light.

Why else? The universe is having a bad day and says you can't. Not even if you say please.

ACTIVITY
Half Speed

See how long you can move your body at half speed. From walking, to lifting your arms and turning your head, move as if you're stuck in some pretty thick pancake syrup. How long can you move at this speed? Pay attention to who gets frustrated first, you or those around you.

> "There would not be any cars and planes because you could go anywhere with that type of speed."
> —Charlie, Oxford Elementary, age 9

ACTIVITY
Speedy To Dos

Take out your journal and fill out a to-do list for tomorrow if, all of a sudden, you could move at the speed of light.

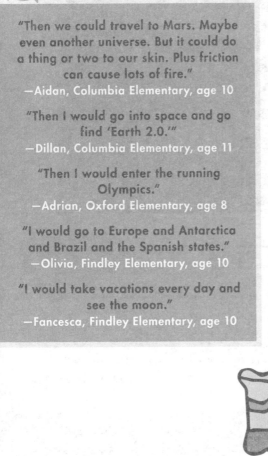

"Then we could travel to Mars. Maybe even another universe. But it could do a thing or two to our skin. Plus friction can cause lots of fire."
—Aidan, Columbia Elementary, age 10

"Then I would go into space and go find 'Earth 2.0.'"
—Dillan, Columbia Elementary, age 11

"Then I would enter the running Olympics."
—Adrian, Oxford Elementary, age 8

"I would go to Europe and Antarctica and Brazil and the Spanish states."
—Olivia, Findley Elementary, age 10

"I would take vacations every day and see the moon."
—Fancesca, Findley Elementary, age 10

What if Humans Ate Insects as Our Primary Source of Food?

You think you're a picky eater now—what if the next pizza you ordered came with grasshoppers, caterpillars, and beetles for toppings? You might find it gross, but nearly a third of the planet eats insects as a part of their daily diet. The practice of eating insects is called entomophagy, and it's done by an estimated 2 billion people![28]

> "Ugh, that would be disgusting, and I don't really want to think about eating bug guts. P.S. Bug blood is green, so if I ate them, there would be green stuff all over my mouth."
> —Ceara, Findley Elementary, age 10
>
> "I tasted an ant, and it was spicy."
> —Aaron, Oxford Elementary, age 10

Not all insect eating has to be a crunchy experience. Some insects, like crickets, are ground up into flour that can then be used to bake cookies. Ready for some fresh-baked chocolate-chip cricket cookies?

Why do people eat insects? Two reasons: they're pretty healthy, and they're everywhere! Your brain may think they're gross, but your body has no problem turning insects into energy. A serving of mealworms has more protein than a serving of chicken.[29]

Another reason people are becoming interested in eating more insects is how environmentally friendly eating them can be. Compared to raising pigs, cows, chickens, and fish, insects take very little food, water, and space.[30]

"Spit them out and go get ice cream."
—Stephen, Findley Elementary, age 9

"Ew. Gross. Disgusting."
—Ervin, Findley Elementary, age 10

"Ick! Insects? Food? I don't think they really go together. But if I was forced to eat insects, and everyone else ate insects too, we would soon run out of food."
—Amy, Findley Elementary, age 9

"That would gross me out. I would never eat again. I don't care—I'd rather starve."
—Nyerie, Oxford Elementary, age 9

What if you're already eating insects? (If you love peanut butter, and you're 100 percent set against ever eating insects, no matter what reasons there might be for doing so, you shouldn't read the next sentence.) The Food and Drug Administration (FDA) allows for an average of thirty or more insect fragments per one hundred grams of peanut butter.[31]

ACTIVITY
Insect Menu

Now that you know you're already eating insects, let's get cooking! Imagine you're going to open the first insect-only restaurant in your neighborhood. Write out a menu in your journal with the soups, salads, main courses, and desserts you'll serve. In addition to giving the ingredients, be sure to name your new dishes.

"I would throw up every day and probably get stung by bugs."
—Olivia, Columbia Elementary, age 10

"Then catching bugs in a net or jar would spell the end of a bug's life and a tasty snack for you."
—Schuyler, Columbia Elementary, age 11

"We would need to eat a lot bigger portions of food because insects are not very filling."
—Cali, Columbia Elementary, age 10

"If we ate insects as our primary source of food, insects would start becoming extinct because there are billions of humans in the world. This would mean we would have to have insect farms everywhere to meet our needs."
—Hilary, Columbia Elementary, age 11

"Then it would help with bug problems."
—Adrian, Oxford Elementary, age 8

"I would like that because I get to try something new."
—Nevaeh, Columbia Elementary, age 11

"Then normal food would taste like worms."
—Carter, Columbia Elementary, age 11

"Then we would get much more protein."
—Daphne, Findley Elementary, age 10

What if You Could Taste and Smell with Your Fingers?

Why should your nose and mouth have all of the fun? You can feel with your entire body, so what if you could experience other senses, like taste and smell, with your entire body? How would your life change? Would you watch what you touched? Would you wear more gloves? Or would you be throwing away all of your forks and spoons?

If you could taste with your fingers, then you could enjoy food without having to eat it, right? What if you could just touch a piece of pizza and get pizza flavor in your mouth? Pretty cool, huh?

As crazy as this "what if" may sound, it's not all that farfetched. Not every animal smells with its nose and tastes with its tongue. For example, snakes smell with their tongues[32] and butterflies taste with their feet[33]!

> "If you could smell with your fingers, people would be much more picky with what they chose to eat."
> —Jaiden, Battle High School, age 16
>
> "Handshakes and high fives, along with other hand contact would be awkward—would it be like kissing them?"
> —Charlie, Battle High School, age 15
>
> "Then when you picked your nose, it would smell really good, and you could say you were smelling your fingers."
> —John Ryan, Battle High School, age 15
>
> "People would have to be super careful wiping their butt."
> —Andrew, Battle High School, age 15

"Gloves would be necessary to go the bathroom, and cook raw food; additionally, any job that requires gloves, such as working with chemicals, would definitely need them now."
—Jonathan, Battle High School, age 17

"I would touch everything."
—Ben, Battle High School, age 17

tasty

What if Humans Only Saw in Black and White?

The world would be a pretty boring place if it were only black and white, right? Would sunsets look as stunning or mountains as majestic if they were seen only in shades of black and white? Imagine how dull a double rainbow would be without all the colors it contains.

Not only do colors convey beauty, they share information. We now use colors to signal certain feelings, warnings, and emotions. Ever wonder why stop signs are red and caution signs yellow? We've been conditioned to respond to certain colors quicker than the words written on them. Many companies and advertisers use colors to their advantage today.

Even though what colors mean today can be similar in most people's minds, the meanings colors hold haven't been the same over time. For example, if someone were to ask you what color a wedding dress is, you (and a lot of other people) would probably say white. But this hasn't always been the case. In European countries alone, the standard color of wedding dresses has been blue, pink, red, even green during different centuries throughout history.[34] If you were to start looking at the colors of wedding dresses from different cultures around the globe, you'd find even more variations. So, while colors can contain meaning, it's usually each of us who create the meaning.

ACTIVITY
Color Match

Look at the names of colors below. Get your journal out and write down the first thing that comes to your mind when you see that color. Then have a friend do the same (but don't let that person see your response!). How many things do you both associate with the same color? If you really want to test this, repeat this with as many people as you can. How often do the same colors make people think of the same things? You might be surprised at how similar your results are.

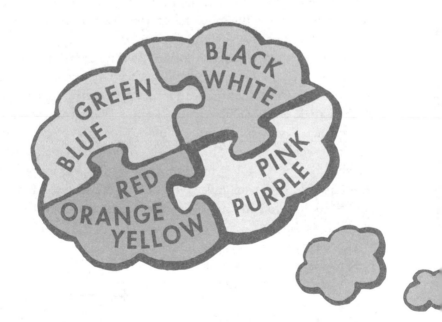

What if Everything Were an Alien Simulation?

Computers get more advanced every day. If you look at video games from 1990, they look very different from those today. We keep adding more ways to interact with games—new controllers and feedback systems. The visual quality is getting significantly better. Virtual worlds are becoming very real.

Some people think that in the future, we will be able to create a video game that is indistinguishable from the real world. We won't even need humans to play it because we could just simulate characters interacting with one another. As long as we have enough resources, we could start simulating a whole bunch of worlds. It would be hundreds and thousands and millions of virtual worlds with virtual people having virtual reactions. So much virtualness!

But what do you think these virtual worlds would *feel* like to the "people" who live there? Since the graphics are so great, and we'd be able to simulate all of our senses, it would probably *feel* real. Even though the inhabitants would be computer-based, they could still think like you and me. They might not even know they were in a simulation.

How many real worlds are there? Just one.

How many virtual worlds would there be? More than anyone can count.

Now, if you had to guess which one you were in, a real world or a virtual world, which would you guess? Chances are you're in a virtual world that feels real. You

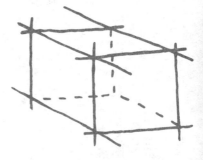

have no way of telling if you're in the year you think you are in. This simulation seems to have started just over 10 billion years ago. But there might be a civilization billions of years older than us that started the simulation.

NICK BOSTROM, PHILOSOPHER

This question is inspired by Nick Bostrom's Simulation Argument. In 2003, he published an article that shows one of three things is true.

1. Almost all civilizations die off before they reach "technological maturity." So, even though we're alive now, our civilization might end before we figure out how to use technology in an entirely responsible way.

2. Once a civilization is able to create hyperreal simulations, people lose interest in it. Even though they are able to do so, the people in the civilization don't create simulations.

3. We are probably living in a simulation.

He doesn't think we have strong evidence for which one of the possibilities is true. Maybe we're the first civilization, the people who will eventually create simulations. Or perhaps we're the first people created by the first computer simulation created by our superintelligent ancestors. Or, even more oddly, maybe we're a simulation that was started by people in a simulation themselves![35]

What if the World of the Small Seemed Very Different from the World of the Big?

Have you ever wondered what happens at the smallest level of the universe? Imagine you zoom in on your hand. Eventually you see all those cracks and ridges of your skin. You keep zooming, and you start to see your cells. Keep going, and you see the parts of your cells, then bands of molecules, then what?

Well, if you keep zooming, you see different parts of a molecule: atoms. Each atom has different amounts of electrons, protons, and neutrons (think about them as particles). Go a little farther into the protons and neutrons and you find elementary particles, things that can't be broken down any farther (though there is debate in the scientific community about this!).

At this level of the universe, things start acting really strange. Particles can tunnel through walls. If this happened at your regular size, you could push against your bedroom wall one hundred times and one of the times fall through the wall. Weird, right? Particles can get entangled with one another. It is kind of like two particles start acting the same, and if you change one, the other changes too. If you got entangled with your friend who then moved to the other side of the world, when one of you changed direction, the other would change direction too. It'd be hard to get anywhere!

SAM DROEGE, USGS BIOLOGIST

You don't have to be as small as an elementary particle to see how the small world is different from yours. Sam Droege is a biologist for the United States Geological Survey (USGS). He also takes high-resolution images of small things, like bees. If you're wandering around outside, you will realize that most bees are too small for you to see clearly. And, even if you're an expert, it's hard to identify most bees because of their small size.[36] Tough luck if you're trying to figure out what is pollinating your plants. That's why you need Droege, because he's the guy with the high-quality bee photos.

At jumbo-size, bees show you all sorts of things: a bee's multipart eyes, their tiny hairs, and even a bunch of pollen. What else do you think we could be missing because we're too large to see it?

TECHNICAL CORNER
Why the Small Is Strange and the Large Is Not

Whoa. This question is really weird. How can the really small stuff in the universe be so strange when, at our size, we never see it? You've never walked through a wall or gotten entangled with a friend. If the tiny things do it, why can't we?!

There's a lot of debate in the scientific community about this. In fact, large things are understood by one kind of math, and the really, really small stuff is understood by a totally different kind of math. Physicists, those people who study physics (how things move and interact), are working to understand the universe with only one type of unified mathematics. You're right. It is weird to have two different things try to describe the same universe. The problem so far has been that, because they describe things quite differently, the two types of math don't really work together very well—yet.

One of the thoughts is that things are just calmer from far away. Think about it like an ocean. If you look at the top of an ocean really close, you see a whole bunch of tiny ripples. But, if you look at the same spot from just a little farther away, the surface seems much calmer. Then, if you look from even farther away, like from a building half a mile inland, the ocean seems even calmer. If you look at the tiniest of particles in the universe, they seem super erratic. But if you look at them from really far away, like on the moon, they seem extremely calm.

What if There Were No Mosquitos?

No mosquitos? What, no slapping your arms during the summer? No more waking up as one big itch? Fantastic!

But did you know that mosquitos are responsible for a lot more problems than red welts filled with pus? These tiny, buzzing insects are one of the world's biggest killers. Because of all that bloodsucking, they also transport deadly diseases from one person or animal to another. Every year, millions of people die from mosquito-borne illnesses.[37]

The world would be a much, much better place if we said good riddance to mosquitos, right? But what about the food chain? Isn't nature in perfect balance? Aren't mosquitos food for larger animals and pollinators for plants that we need? If all of the mosquitos were gone, it would start a spiral effect of catastrophe, right?

What if it wouldn't? Unlike other tiny nuisances (like bees) in our ecosystem, whose disappearance would spell disaster, mosquitos could disappear— many scientists don't foresee any problems with wiping out mosquitos. In fact, the only problem they can think of is, without millions of people dying from mosquitos every year, we might have too many people on the planet.[38]

> "The world would rejoice. The amount of diseases, especially in developing nations, would reduce. Also unlike other insects, mosquitoes are not integral to maintain biodiversity."
> —Jonathan, Battle High School, age 17

So, what if there were no mosquitos? Well, we'd have a new question to ponder: What if there were too many people on the planet? Which question would you rather find an answer to?

ACTIVITY
Food Web

Everything in the environment is connected. Choose a plant or animal and find out how it is connected to other plants and animals. Make a food web in your journal by drawing branches from your first choice to the new plants and animals you find. Each plant or animal is a node and each connection is a connection (pretty straightforward, right?). Keep working until you have a few loops on which, if you follow a connection away from one node, eventually you get back to your original node.

"Then fishing and hunting would be way easier."
—John Ryan, Battle High School, age 15

"The spread of disease would be significantly lessened, but mosquito-eating animals wouldn't have their food."
—Madi, Battle High School, age 15

What if All the Continents Were Joined Together?

What if there were a single "supercontinent"? What if, at one time in the Earth's history, there was? Roughly 270 million years ago, most of the Earth's landmass was huddled up together in one continent called Pangaea. Around 200 million years ago, the Earth's shifting plates started breaking this continent up, and huge masses of land started drifting across the oceans until they reached where they are now. They haven't stopped moving, either. If you've ever felt an earthquake before, it was the side effect of the Earth's shifting plates.

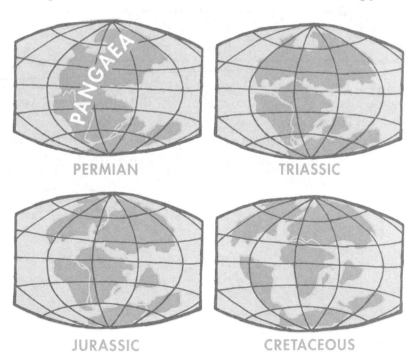

PERMIAN

TRIASSIC

JURASSIC

CRETACEOUS

Even though the location of the Earth's continents probably won't change enough in your lifetime to require you to order a World Map 2.0, the Earth is always moving. Pangaea wasn't the first or only supercontinent. In fact, scientists who study the Earth's movements believe our current continents are moving toward forming yet another supercontinent in the very distant future.[39]

Aside from the geographic changes involved with a single continent, what other changes do you think would happen if there were no oceans to separate all the humans on the planet? Would we have the diversity of cultures we have now, or would we share a single culture? Would there be more wars, or fewer? How about the history of science and learning? What if, instead of all of the smartest people studying and experimenting far away from each other, they could have worked together? What would the world look like today if it had never broken up in the past?

ACTIVITY
Earth Puzzle

What if the Earth's continents and countries were a bunch of puzzle pieces, and you got to reconstruct the Earth however you wanted? Draw a new map with new borders and locations for the Earth's countries and continents.

What if You Could Turn into an Animal?

Let's be honest, being a human being can be boring sometimes. Other animals get to climb on ceilings, soar through the air, live underwater, have claws, etc., while we humans must walk around on the ground with soft hands and very, very little fur. But we do have a supercomputer for a brain, so why not use it? Among other things, this brain allows us to wonder and ask, "What if . . . ?"

So, what if you could turn into an animal? What would be the biggest improvement you would experience while being an animal over being a human? What would be your biggest danger, threat, or disadvantage? Would there be things you could no longer do? Would there be other creatures trying to eat you? How would you survive?

Now that you're imagining yourself as an animal, what would be the first thing you do? Can you think of anything you might miss the most about not being human? Would you interact with humans? Why or why not? How? What would you tell animals about humans?

ACTIVITY
Animal You!

Draw a picture of the animal you and your new home. Where would you live? What would you eat? Who would be your friends?

What if Everything Were a Hyperlink?

Do you know where your clothes come from? What about your computers or the paper in this book?

Today, our objects get worked on from people and machines all around the world. The cotton in your shirt might have been picked in China, processed in India, woven into fabric in Vietnam, sewn together into a shirt in Brazil, packaged and sent to a warehouse in Canada, and then sent to the store you bought it from. Look at all the objects around you. They are made up of components made in different places, shipped to different places. And now, they sit quietly around you.

If everything were a hyperlink, you'd be able to investigate all the objects around you. You'd be able to learn who (or which robot) built your phone or where your food came from. If you could learn more about these, would you? Would you be interested to know the journey of all of your things?

ACTIVITY
Hyper It Up

Create a word web of ideas in your journal. Start by writing one word in the middle of a page. Then, draw five branches off it, and at the end of each branch, write a word that is related to your core word. Do that again for each of your new words. Cool. Now, do it one more time. You should have a whole bunch of words and lines connecting them. Finish your drawing by connecting any of the words that are related but don't have lines connecting them yet.

VANNEVAR BUSH, TED NELSON, AND DOUGLAS ENGELBART: THE ORIGINATORS OF HYPERMEDIA

Three guys helped start the idea of hypertext and other hypermedia: Vannevar Bush, Ted Nelson, and Douglas Engelbart. If you're at a birthday party and people ask, "What is hypermedia and who originated it?" you can inform them: "Hypermedia is a group of objects, a group of links, and a way to move between the objects through links. It's connected information that could be text, audio, video, or other things that hold information." You're surely going to be the coolest kid at the party. Well . . . you'll at least be the most informed about hypermedia.

Vannevar Bush had this idea of something called a memex. It's a device that allows you to explore your personal (mental) objects and links. Years later, Ted Nelson came around and created the actual term *hypertext*. He was thinking about how when people use *hyper-*, they are trying to extend whatever word *hyper* is connected to. So, hypertext would be text that goes beyond words on a page or screen. Around the same time, Douglas Engelbart was thinking about computers, people, and how the heck we were going to interact with each other. He realized that we both need a language, something that organizes and structures our thoughts about the world. That language, he thought, was hypertext: words and ideas connected by links. These links could be from ideas being connected or by the words themselves. Any way you look back, you'll connect to these three as the early formers of hypertext.[40]

What if You Had a Superpower?

What would your superpower (only one!) be and why? Mask or no mask? Would you have a secret identity or not? Cape or no cape? Would you rather be part machine like Iron Man or have "naturally" freaky powers like Spider-Man?

Science is constantly coming up with new ways to improve the human body. From creating new medicine to help the body function better, to designing electronic devices to put inside you, scientists are helping us become more and more "super" every day. What if there were an entire world of Hulks or Iron Men walking around?

Imagine what you could do if you were part machine? What if your legs were powered by electricity? How fast would you be able to run? What if you could pick up anything and everything?

Ever wish you had a super brain? What if you could download a book directly into your brain instead of having to read—or remember—it? What if you could be invisible? Sound crazy? Not to the scientists who are currently creating invisibility cloaks for soldiers and working on turning many other "powers" from the pages of comic books into reality. As long as we define *superpower* as an ability to do something a "normal" human body cannot do, we're all about to become a lot less "normal."

Not everybody needs to have special new parts to gain superpowers. Some are born with amazing abilities. Just look at these interesting humans born with "super" powers.

- Michel Lotito can eat anything, including an airplane!

- Ben Underwood used echolocation instead of sight.

- Tim Cridland can feel no pain.

- Mas Oyama (born Choi Yeong-Eui) was a super fighter who could kill bulls and bears with his bare hands.

> "It would be something lame, like Hindsight Lad, who has the ability to tell you how something would have worked out much better if something different happened, in hindsight."
> —Charlie, Battle High School, age 15

Can you find downsides to having some of these superpowers? For instance, if you can't feel pain, how will you know your stovetop is on when you accidentally put your hand on a burner?

ACTIVITY
Create the Super You

Take out your journal and draw your new super identity. What is your superpower? What is your weakness? What would your superhero costume look like? Who is your arch nemesis? What do you fight for (e.g., truth, justice, and the American way)?

What if You Could Explore
Outer Space?

Space is a big place. There is a lot of room between stars and planets. There is so much room between objects in space that it can take many, many years for light to travel from one galaxy to the next. When you're outside at night, looking up at the stars, do you ever wonder what is up there?

The first question is, where do you want to go? Do you want to travel to see new stars? Look at new galaxies? Do you want to find new planets and moons? Are you looking for plants and animals too? What kinds of creatures do you think you'll find on alien planets? Do you think they'll be smarter than us? More or less advanced?

What kinds of plants would you find? Which plants grow and how they grow depends on the environment they are in. Trees that are in environments with more carbon dioxide grow larger. Some plants thrive in the sun while others can live only in shade. What new environments will you find?

The next question is, how are you going to get to your destination? You can get on a spaceship. But since the nearest galaxy is forty-two thousand light-years away,[41] it will take you forty-two thousand years—if you are traveling at the speed of light. If you're traveling for that long, you should bring more than a sleeping bag. Hopefully hibernation technology comes around, and you can sleep or be frozen the whole trip. And hopefully humanity will be here when you get back, or who will you share your discoveries with?

ACTIVITY
Sagittarius or Bust

Draw where you would go and what it would look like. You could even print pictures out and paste them together to create the new landscape.

ELON MUSK, ENTREPRENEUR

NASA, essentially the United States' space exploration group, has lost a percentage of its funding, making it harder to explore space. After selling PayPal, Elon Musk started a company called SpaceX. According to its mission, "SpaceX designs, manufactures and launches advanced rockets and spacecraft. The company was founded in 2002 to revolutionize space technology, with the ultimate goal of enabling people to live on other planets."[42] Why should we go to other planets? Musk thinks that there are a few things that fit on an evolutionary scale: single-cell organisms, differentiation of plants and animals, life moving from oceans to land, mammals, consciousness, and finally life becoming multiplanetary. That's the first part. The second part is that if something is important enough to be put in the history of evolution, maybe we should put some of our resources toward achieving it.[43]

What if You Could Engineer at Planetary Proportions?

You might have heard of engineers. They are the people who build highly technical structures like medical devices, bridges, skyscrapers, robots, spaceships, submarines, traffic systems, and nuclear power plants. They solve problems and build things precisely.

The Burj Khalifa, the tallest building in the world at 2,716.5 feet,[44] is still miniscule in comparison to the size of the Earth. Really, anything engineers build is pretty small. But there are now a few engineers who are trying to engineer our whole planet.

Realizing we might have to take drastic measures to stop climate change, some engineers have been thinking about clouds. If part of the problem with the climate is that too much heat is getting trapped in the Earth's atmosphere, what could we do to reduce the amount of heat coming in? Light from the sun comes in through our atmosphere and warms what it hits. But since only some of the sun's light makes it through the clouds and the rest bounces back into space, the Earth heats up less than it would without clouds. These cloud engineers are finding ways of creating both more clouds and more reflective clouds.[45]

Other engineers are working on plans to help the algae in the oceans grow, thereby reducing the amount of carbon in the atmosphere and reducing the planet's ability to hold extra heat.[46] Even though plans are being made and experiments are being performed, nothing major has been implemented. Since geoengineering affects all of us, scientists take lots of precautions.

ACTIVITY
What Would You Build That Was the Size of a Planet?

Planets are pretty big. If you could build something that big, what would you build? Or if you could change Earth, how would you change it? Draw pictures and write in your journal.

WANGARI MAATHAI, DRIVEN ENVIRONMENTALIST

You don't have to be a geoengineer to change the world's climate. With a PhD in veterinary anatomy and a background in biology, Wangari Maathai started an organization called the Green Belt Movement.[47] She saw that other women in Kenya were losing their food supply and water resources, and had to walk farther and farther to get firewood. Maathai started the Green Belt Movement with a simple, yet powerful idea: trees help keep the "soil [together], store rainwater, and provide food and firewood," so let's plant some trees.[48]

In the years since its foundation in 1977, Maathai's organization has helped rural Kenyan women plant trees to better their own communities. And, in 2004, she received a Nobel Peace Prize for her work.[49] Maathai wanted to make the world a better place. She found a simple idea that resonated with others, and then she helped that idea spread in order to change her community.

What if You Experienced the Unknown?

You have five senses. You can see, smell, hear, taste, and touch. Everywhere you go, you bring these senses with you, to experience the world. But what if there is more than what you can experience?

Take sight. We see reds, blues, greens, purples, and all sorts of colors—what physicists call visible light. What we see is part of a larger spectrum of electromagnetism. X-rays, microwaves, ultraviolet light, radio waves, and infrared light are also on the spectrum, but we just can't see them! Some bugs see ultraviolet light, and to them, flowers are very different colors than they are to us.

Hearing is similar. We can hear up to a certain high pitch and down to a certain low pitch. If you have a dog, you might have noticed it can hear more than you can.

It's hard to imagine what other colors of light would look like or what sounds are beyond what we can hear. What if we were to change our senses even more?

Think about your eyes. They have been looking forward out of the front of your head for your entire life. They help you walk around and guide your hands. Your brain is used to them. What if you could move your eyes outside of your body? Weird! You might be able to hold one eye in each of your hands and move it around independently. You could look around corners just by rolling your eyes around the corner.

You could also put your eyes really close to the ground to feel like one of your pets. Or you could put your eyes really high in the sky to be like a bird. You could put your eyes a few feet above your head and behind you such that it would be like you're playing a third-person video game when you walk around. You could put your eyes in the back of your head so you could see behind you. You could flip your eyes upside down to flip the world upside down (but remember, you'd still be standing upright). You could put your eyes into special lenses that would allow you to see all around you at the same time. You could put your eyes on a wall and walk around a room as though you were seeing out of a fly's eyes!

It doesn't even have to be sight that you're extending. What if you could feel via touch if you were going to get sick? Or what if your big toe vibrated when someone was calling you?

ACTIVITY
Real Surrealism

What would you do if you could remove your eyes from your head? Where would you put them? What would you want to experience if you could experience more?

Conclusion

Thank you! You've hung out with us through a book full of questions, activities, and interviews. You're officially a curious person. Boom! The book is running out of pages, but that doesn't mean the curiosity has to be over.

Now it's on you to go out into your world and ask deep questions —or silly ones! No matter how the question starts, finding an answer can take you to different edges of your mind and the world.

A question is a powerful thing!

Empires have been built on questions, and they've fallen with questions. It's OK to not know the answer sometimes. We don't always know. Even the experts had to start somewhere. Don't be nervous—be proud that you're courageous enough to question everything!

The questions in this book shouldn't just spur deeper thinking —they should spur conversations. Conversations can change the world—especially when those conversations turn into actions. That's where the power of this book lies: in its ability to spur and further conversations about difficult and new subjects so that we may cocreate a better future.

If you'd like to get connected with a global community of What Iffers who are already working together to turn big ideas into even bigger actions, go to whatif360.com to learn more. You'll also be able to explore the questions people have asked in the past, find an event near you, or even sign up to speak at a What If . . . ? 360 Experience.

We're looking forward to hearing your world-shaking question!

We'd also love to bring a What If . . . ? 360 Experience to your school, so you can join the other schools around the world turning ideas into actions by asking, "What if . . . ?"

If you use social media, you can find us on Facebook, Twitter, YouTube, and Google+.

#WhatIf360

Facebook: facebook.com/TheWhatIfConference

Twitter: @WhatIf_360

Google+: What If . . . ? 360

YouTube: youtube.com/TheWhatIfConference

We'd Like to Say Thanks

What if there are far too many people to thank than could possibly fit in the pages of this book? For a start, though, I'd like to thank my agent, Jessica Regel, who has been helping me make my dream of becoming a writer come true over and over again. I'd also like to thank our editors, Lindsay Easterbrooks-Brown, Emmalisa Sparrow, and Kristin Thiel at Beyond Words, for believing enough in the power of asking, "What if . . . ?" to help us put it on some pages between a couple covers so we could share it with the world. I'd also like to thank the ever-growing global community of What Iffers who refuse to accept the way things are and continue to commit their thoughts and actions to cocreating a better world, not just for tomorrow but for today. Thank you! Lastly, I'd like to thank my wife, Seung Ah Lee, for putting up with all my craziness. That is all.

—Matt

Thanks to everyone who stuck with us on both the What If . . . ? journey and our personal ones. Thanks to our editors, Lindsay Easterbrooks-Brown, Emmalisa Sparrow, and Kristin Thiel, for helping us craft and realize our vision. Thanks to our agent, Jess Regel, for advising us along the way. Thanks to my mother, Stephanie McHugh, for helping me through tough times. Thanks to my various clients and employers for such a flexible schedule while I was writing. Thanks to my friends who have provided feedback and shot me resources, especially to Caroline Slavin for her Ada Byron spotlight suggestion. Thanks to Ben Cairns for helping edit early drafts of the book. Thanks to Dr. Selcen Phelps, a dear friend and always-mentor. Thanks to each of my teachers; you were the reasons I was able to

write well about so many things. And a special thanks to my partner Abby Stokes for her continued encouragement, support, edits
of drafts, feedback, interview transcriptions, resource locating, and
citation formatting. Finally, thanks to all of you for picking up a copy
of this book and helping active curiosity thrive.

—Andrew

Notes

Special note: All kid answers were collected in the months of September 2014, January 2015, and April 2015. These students came from a variety of places, from Columbia Elementary in Bellingham, Washington, and Oxford Elementary School in Berkeley, California, to Findley Elementary School in Beaverton, Oregon, and Battle High School in Columbia, Missouri. All of these kids rock!

Special note #2: Though none of our material was taken directly from *What If. . . ?: Collected Thought Experiments in Philosophy* by Peg Tittle, we referenced this book to remind ourselves of many of the questions that ended up in our own book. *What If. . . ?* directed us to some of the sources cited, saving us a good chunk of time.

History

1. "Top 10 Misconceptions about Dinosaurs," Smithsonian National Museum of Natural History, accessed September 1, 2014, http://paleobiology.si.edu /dinosaurs/info/misconceptions/mis_4.html.

2. "Dinosaur FAQ," Smithsonian National Museum of Natural History, accessed September 1, 2014, http://paleobiology.si.edu/dinosaurs/info/faq /faq_2.html.

3. Ibid.

4. DinoBuzz: Current Topics Concerning Dinosaurs, "Are Birds Really Dinosaurs?," University of California Museum of Paleontology, last modified January 22, 1998, http://www.ucmp.berkeley.edu/diapsids/avians.html.

5. Ben Waggoner, "Mary Anning (1799-1847)," University of California Museum of Paleontology, accessed August 10, 2015, http://www.ucmp .berkeley.edu/history/anning.html.

6. Invictus, "The Mongol Empire," All Empires Online History Community, last modified February 2007, http://www.allempires.com/article/?q=The _Mongol_Empire.

7. Abby Rogers, "The 10 Greatest Empires in the History of the World," *Business Insider*, November 9, 2011, http://www.businessinsider.com /the-10-greatest-empires-in-history-2011-9#2-the-mongol-empire-was-the -largest-contiguous-empire-the-world-has-ever-seen-9.

8. Crash Course World History, "Wait for It . . . The Mongols!," YouTube video, 11:32, posted by CrashCourse, May 17, 2012, https://www.youtube.com /watch?v=szxParOBcMo.

9. Rebecca Brayton, "The History of the Mongol Empire," WatchMojo.com video, 2:50, May 23, 2010, http://www.watchmojo.com/video/id/8258.

10. Evan Andrews, "10 Things You May Not Know about Genghis Khan," History.com, April 29, 2014, http://www.history.com/news/history-lists /10-things-you-may-not-know-about-genghis-khan.

11. Hillary Mayell, "Genghis Khan a Prolific Lover, DNA Data Implies," *National Geographic News*, February 14, 2003, http://news.national geographic.com/news/2003/02/0214_030214_genghis.html.

12. "How Did America Get Its Name?," Library of Congress, August 2003, http://www.loc.gov/wiseguide/aug03/america.html.

13. Ibid.

14. Mat Barkhausen, "Native Americans Influenced American Political Thought," PowWows.com, September 29, 2011, http://www.powwows .com/2011/09/29/native-americans-influenced-american-political-thought.

15. David Yarrow, "The Great Law of Peace: New World Roots of American Democracy," Kahonwes.com, September 1987, http://www.kahonwes.com /iroquois/document1.html.

16. Cristen Conger, "10 NASA Inventions You Might Use Every Day," Long Beach Unified School District, accessed September 1, 2014, http://www .lbschools.net/Main_Offices/Curriculum/Areas/English_Language_Arts /docs/Common_Core/14-15/NASA%20inventions.pdf.

17. Claire Suddath, "A Brief History of: Velcro," *Time*, June 15, 2010, http:// content.time.com/time/nation/article/0,8599,1996883,00.html.

18. Conger, "10 NASA Inventions."

19. Ibid.

20. "Neil deGrasse Tyson—We Stopped Dreaming (Episode 1)," YouTube video, 5:19, posted by "Evan Schurr," March 9, 2012, http://youtu.be /CbIZU8cQWXc.

21. "Neil deGrasse Tyson: On the First Moon Landing," YouTube video, 7:24, posted by "Alfonso J. Ramos," July 28, 2012, https://www.youtube.com/watch ?v=Q6ClA5f5uu0.

22. "Neil deGrasse Tyson," Hayden Planetarium, accessed November 1, 2014, http://www.haydenplanetarium.org/tyson/profile/about-neil-degrasse-tyson.

23. Tom Benson, "Brief History of Rockets," NASA, last modified June 12, 2014, http://www.grc.nasa.gov/WWW/k-12/TRC/Rockets/history_of _rockets.html.

24. Michio Kaku, *Physics of the Impossible: A Scientific Exploration into the World of Phasers, Force Fields, Teleportation, and Time Travel* (New York: Doubleday, 2008).

25. Michio Kaku, *Hyperspace: A Scientific Odyssey through Parallel Universes, Time Warps, and the 10th Dimension* (New York: Doubleday, 1994).

26. Ibid.

27. David Toomey, *The New Time Travelers: A Journey to the Frontiers of Physics* (New York: W. W. Norton & Company, 2007).

28. James Gleick, *The Information* (New York: Pantheon Books, 2011), 38–39.

29. Rachel Grate, "Science Has Great News for People Who Read Actual Books," Arts.Mic, September 22, 2014, http://mic.com/articles/99408 /science-has-great-news-for-people-who-read-actual-books.

30. Alison Flood, "Readers Absorb Less on Kindles than on Paper, Study Finds," *The Guardian*, August 19, 2014, http://www.theguardian.com /books/2014/aug/19/readers-absorb-less-kindles-paper-study-plot -ereader-digitisation.

31. Grate, "Science Has Great News."

32. "Vision / Strategy," Seasteading Institute, accessed October 27, 2015, http://www.seasteading.org/about/vision-strategy/.

33. "Floating City Project," Seasteading Institute, accessed January 10, 2015, http://www.seasteading.org/floating-city-project.

34. Jonathan Miles, "The Billionaire King of Techtopia," *Details*, September 1, 2011, http://www.details.com/culture-trends/critical-eye/201109/peter-thiel -billionaire-paypal-facebook-internet-success.

35. "FAQ," Seasteading Institute, accessed January 12, 2015, http://www
.seasteading.org/about/faq.

36. "About," Seasteading Institute, accessed January 12, 2015, http://www
.seasteading.org/about.

37. "About the Fellowship," Thiel Fellowship, accessed January 10, 2015, http://
www.thielfellowship.org/about/about-the-fellowship.

38. "The Six States," Six Californias, accessed January 12, 2015, http://www
.sixcalifornias.com/the_six_states.

39. Joel Stein, "Billionaire Tim Draper's Mad Plan to Blow Up California,"
Bloomberg Businessweek, July 31, 2014, http://www.businessweek.com
/articles/2014-07-31/six-californias-a-tim-draper-idea-just-as-madcap-as
-the-others.

40. Ibid.

41. "About," Six Californias, accessed January 12, 2015, http://www
.sixcalifornias.com/about.

42. "About Draper University," Draper University, accessed January 12, 2015,
http://draperuniversity.com/about.

43. "America's 10 Deadliest Wars," MarketWatch, May 25, 2014, http://www
.marketwatch.com/story/americas-10-deadliest-wars-2014-05-23.

44. Mark Juddery, "What If? 19 Alternate Histories Imagining a Very
Different World," *Mental Floss*, January 9, 2014, http://mentalfloss.com
/article/54464/what-if-19-alternate-histories-imagining-very-different-world.

45. Ernest B. Furgurson, "Churchill Imagines How the South Won the Civil
War," *HistoryNet.com*, August 3, 2011, http://www.historynet.com/churchill
-imagines-how-the-south-won-the-civil-war.htm.

46. Gary Gene Fuenfhausen, "Missouri's Little Dixie," LittleDixie.net, January
2009, http://littledixie.net.

47. "Once You Know . . . Fulton, Missouri: History," City of Fulton, accessed
January 9, 2015, http://fultonmo.org/once-you-know/history.

48. "Milestones: 1776–1783: French Alliance, French Assistance, and
European Diplomacy during the American Revolution, 1778–1782," US
Department of State, Office of the Historian, accessed January 8, 2015, https://
history.state.gov/milestones/1776-1783/french-alliance.

49. "Milestones: 1776–1783: Benjamin Franklin: First American Diplomat,
1776–1785," US Department of State, Office of the Historian, accessed
January 8, 2015, https://history.state.gov/milestones/1776-1783/b-franklin.

50. "World War II History," History.com, accessed January 10, 2015, http://www.history.com/topics/world-war-ii/world-war-ii-history.

51. "An Interview with General Otto Ernst Remer," by Stephanie Shoeman, trans. Mark Weber, *Journal of Historical Review* 10, no. 1 (Spring 1990): 108–117, http://www.ihr.org/jhr/v10/v10p108_Schoeman.html.

52. Timothy Snyder, "How Hitler Could Have Won," *New York Times Sunday Book Review*, June 17, 2011, http://www.nytimes.com/2011/06/19/books/review/book-review-the-storm-of-war-a-new-history-of-the-second-world-war-by-andrew-roberts.html?_r=0.

53. "Joseph Stalin," National Cold War Exhibition, accessed January 10, 2015, http://www.nationalcoldwarexhibition.org/the-cold-war/biographies/joseph-stalin/ (page discontinued).

54. Palash Ghosh, "How Many People Did Joseph Stalin Kill?," *International Business Times*, March 5, 2013, http://www.ibtimes.com/how-many-people-did-joseph-stalin-kill-1111789.

55. Nigel Jones, "From Stalin to Hitler, the Most Murderous Regimes in the World," *Mail Online*, October 7, 2014, http://www.dailymail.co.uk/home/moslive/article-2091670/Hitler-Stalin-The-murderous-regimes-world.html.

56. "Joseph Stalin," National Cold War Exhibition.

57. Daniel R. Headrick, *When Information Came of Age: Technologies of Knowledge in the Age of Reason and Revolution, 1700–1850* (New York: Oxford University Press, 2000), 217.

58. Gerard J. Holzmann and Björn Pehrson, *The Early History of Data Networks* (Los Alamitos, CA: IEEE Computer Society Press, 1995), 51.

59. Headrick, *When Information Came of Age*, 156–157.

60. Rus Shuler, "How Does the Internet Work?," last modified 2002, http://web.stanford.edu/class/msande91si/www-spr04/readings/week1/InternetWhitepaper.htm.

61. "George Lucas on Mentors and Faith," *Moyers & Company*, August 9, 2012, http://billmoyers.com/2012/08/09/moyers-moment-1999-george-lucas-on-mentors-and-faith.

62. Steve Persall, "Move Over, Odysseus, Here Comes Luke Skywalker," *St. Petersburg Times*, 1999, http://www.folkstory.com/articles/petersburg.html.

63. Joseph Campbell, *A Joseph Campbell Companion: Reflections on the Art of Living*, (San Anselmo, CA: Joseph Campbell Foundation, 2011), Kindle eBook, "In the Field."

64. Joseph Campbell and Bill D. Moyers, *The Power of Myth* (New York: Doubleday, 1988).

65. Kevin Kelly, *What Technology Wants* (New York: Penguin Group, 2010), 11.

66. Ibid, 272.

67. Steven Johnson, *Where Good Ideas Come From: The Natural History of Innovation* (New York: Riverhead, 2010).

68. Ray Kurzweil, *The Age of Spiritual Machines: When Computers Exceed Human Intelligence* (New York: Penguin Group, 2000).

69. "Nikola Tesla's Idea of Wireless Transmission of Electrical Energy Is a Solution for World Energy Crisis," Tesla Memorial Society of New York, accessed September 1, 2014, http://www.teslasociety.com/tesla_tower.htm.

70. "Tesla: Life and Legacy—Tower of Dreams," PBS, accessed June 25, 2015, http://www.pbs.org/tesla/ll/ll_todre.html.

71. Ljubo Vujovic, "Tesla Biography: Nikola Tesla, the Genius Who Lit the World," Tesla Memorial Society of New York, July 10, 1998, http://www.teslasociety.com/biography.htm.

72. Ibid.

73. Ibid.

People

1. Arghavan Salles, "Ephemeroptera: Mayflies," University of California Museum of Paleontology, August 4, 2000, http://www.ucmp.berkeley.edu/arthropoda/uniramia/ephemeroptera.html.

2. "Births and Natality," Centers for Disease Control and Prevention, last modified May 14, 2015, http://www.cdc.gov/nchs/fastats/births.htm.

3. Aubrey de Grey, interview by Andrew R McHugh, September 13, 2014.

4. Aubrey D. N. J. de Grey, "Ending Aging," YouTube video, 1:05:13, from Talks at Google on April 7, 2014, posted by Talks at Google, April 11, 2014, https://www.youtube.com/watch?v=tXJzvo0Jekc.

5. Stephen W. Stathis, "Federal Holidays: Evolution and Application," CRS Report for Congress, last modified February 8, 1999, http://www.senate.gov/reference/resources/pdf/Federal_Holidays.pdf.

6. Ibid.

7. Peter Tyson, "Bear Essentials of Hibernation," *NOVA*, December 18, 2000, http://www.pbs.org/wgbh/nova/nature/bear-essentials-of-hibernation.html.

8. Ibid.

9. "Fun Hibernation Facts," Scholastic, accessed September 1, 2014, http://www.scholastic.com/teachers/article/fun-hibernation-facts.

10. Nola Taylor Redd, "How Long Does It Take to Get to Mars?," Space.com, February 13, 2014, http://www.space.com/24701-how-long-does-it-take-to-get-to-mars.html.

11. "World's Largest Digging Machine Is Huge," *Geekologie*, August 19, 2008, http://www.geekologie.com/2008/08/worlds-largest-digging-machine.php.

12. Ariel Schwartz, "10 Jobs That You Could Have in 2030," *Co.Exist*, June 2, 2014, http://www.fastcoexist.com/3031225/futurist-forum/10-jobs-that-you-could-have-in-2030.

13. Sugata Mitra, "The Child-Driven Education," TEDGlobal 2010, 17:13, filmed July 2010, https://www.ted.com/talks/sugata_mitra_the_child_driven_education.

14. Vinod Khosla, "Technology Will Replace 80% of What Doctors Do," *Fortune*, December 4, 2012, http://fortune.com/2012/12/04/technology-will-replace-80-of-what-doctors-do.

15. "A Futurist on Why Lawyers Will Start Becoming Obsolete This Year," *Wired*, March 28, 2014, http://www.wired.com/2014/03/geeks-guide-karl-schroeder.

16. Paul Ingrassia, "Look, No Hands! Test Driving a Google Car," *Reuters*, August 17, 2014, http://www.reuters.com/article/2014/08/17/us-google-driverless-idUSKBN0GH02P20140817

17. M. Paul Lewis, Gary F. Simons, and Charles D. Fennig, eds., *Ethnologue: Languages of the World*, 17th ed. (Dallas: SIL International, 2014).

18. Ibid.

19. Ibid.

20. Suzanne Kemmer, "Major Periods of Borrowing," Rice University, accessed September 1, 2014, http://www.ruf.rice.edu/~kemmer/Words04/structure/borrowed.html.

21. Mark Rice-Oxley, "The Germans Have a Word for It—And It's a Very Long One," *The Guardian*, September 21, 2012, http://www.theguardian.com/world/2012/sep/21/germans-word-long-language.

22. Ker Than, "L. L. Zamenhof: Who He Was, Why He's on Google," *National Geographic News,* December 15, 2009, http://news.nationalgeographic.com/news/2009/12/091215-ll-zamenhof-google-doodle-esperanto-150th-birthday.html.

23. "Five Fun Facts about Esperanto," *Bloomsbury Linguistics* (blog), Bloomsbury Academic, May 22, 2014, http://bloomsburylinguistics.typepad .com/continuum-linguistics/2014/05/five-fun-facts-about-esperanto.html.

24. Jonathan Jenkins Ichikawa and Matthias Steup, "The Analysis of Knowledge," *The Stanford Encyclopedia of Philosophy*, Spring 2014 ed., last modified November 15, 2012, http://plato.stanford.edu/archives/spr2014 /entries/knowledge-analysis.

25. Jane Jacobs, *The Death and Life of Great American Cities* (New York: Modern Library, 2011), 440–484.

26. "Jane Jacobs," Project for Public Spaces, accessed January 10, 2014, http:// www.pps.org/reference/jjacobs-2.

27. Adi Robertson, "Scientists Turn Dreams into Eerie Short Films with an MRI Scan," *Verge*, April 4, 2013, http://www.theverge.com/2013/4/4/4184728 /scientists-decode-dreams-with-mri-scan.

28. "Profile: Malala Yousafzai," *BBC News*, December 10, 2014, http://www .bbc.com/news/world-asia-23241937.

29. "Malala and Kailash Satyarthi Win Nobel Peace Prize," *BBC News*, October 10, 2014, http://www.bbc.com/news/world-europe-29564935.

30. Kathryn Schulz, "On Being Wrong," TED2011, 17:51, filmed March 2011, http://www.ted.com/talks/kathryn_schulz_on_being_wrong.

31. James Gleick, *The Information: A History, a Theory, a Flood* (New York: Pantheon Books, 2011), 106.

32. Ibid., 111.

33. Ibid., 104–105.

34. Ibid., 116.

35. Thomas Hobbes, "Of Identity and Difference," *The English Works of Thomas Hobbes of Malmesbury*, vol. 1 (London: John Bohn, 1839), Part II, 136–138, http://books.google.com/books?id=Gr8LAAAAIAAJ.

36. David Eagleman, interview by Andrew R McHugh, October 21, 2014.

37. "The Woman Who Designed The Swoosh," Women You Should Know, June 12, 2012, http://www.womenyoushouldknow.net/the-woman-who -designed-the-swoosh/.

38. Kaku, *Physics of the Impossible*, 62.

39. Alexander Osterwalder, "Why I Want My Kids to Fail," *Business Innovation Factory* video, 17:06, 2010, http://www.businessinnovationfactory.com

/summit/video/alexander-osterwalder-why-i-want-my-kids-fail
#.VI4yhGTF-m0.

40. Alexander Osterwalder and Yves Pigneur, *Business Model Generation: A Handbook for Visionaries, Game Changers, and Challengers* (Hoboken, NJ: John Wiley & Sons, 2010).

41. Osterwalder, "Why I Want My Kids to Fail."

42. Alexis Ohanian, *Without Their Permission: How the 21st Century Will Be Made, Not Managed* (New York: Hachette Book Group, 2013).

Stuff

1. "Nanorobotics," *ScienceDaily*, accessed January 8, 2015, http://www.sciencedaily.com/articles/n/nanorobotics.htm.

2. "Particle Sizes," Engineering ToolBox, accessed January 8, 2015, http://www.engineeringtoolbox.com/particle-sizes-d_934.html.

3. "Size and Scale," UW MRSEC Education Group, last modified May 20, 2015, http://education.mrsec.wisc.edu/36.htm.

4. Ibid.

5. Jason Dorrier, "Can DNA Nanobots Successfully Treat Cancer Patients? First Human Trial Soon," Singularity HUB, January 8, 2015, http://singularityhub.com/2015/01/08/can-dna-nanobots-successfully-treat-cancer-patient-first-human-trial-soon/#.VK8coaCxTvY.facebook.

6. "Cellular Surgeons: The New Era of Nanomedicine," YouTube video, 1:27:59, posted by Word Science Festival, August 1, 2014, https://youtu.be/FzFY5ms3AUc.

7. Alex Madinger, interview by Andrew R McHugh, September 11, 2014.

8. Amber Case, interview by Andrew R McHugh, September 19, 2014.

9. GPS.gov, "How GPS Works," accessed November 1, 2014, http://www.gps.gov/multimedia/poster/poster-web.pdf.

10. Sherry Turkle, *Alone Together: Why We Expect More from Technology and Less from Each Other* (New York: Basic Books, 2011).

11. Ibid.

12. Dr. K. Gudmundsson, "The Many Uses of Nanobots," Enlil Science DBD Research Institute, accessed January 8, 2015, http://dbdresearchinstitute.com/the-many-uses-of-nanobots (page discontinued).

13. Ibid.

14. Lawrence Osborne, "The Gray-Goo Problem," *New York Times*, December 14, 2003, http://www.nytimes.com/2003/12/14/magazine/14GRAY.html.

15. CMStewart, "Our Grey Goo Future: Possibility and Probability," *Singularity* (blog), January 6, 2012, https://www.singularityweblog.com/our-grey-goo -future-possibility-and-probability.

16. Patrick Farrell and Kassie Bracken, "A Tiny Fruit That Tricks the Tongue," *New York Times*, May 28, 2008, http://www.nytimes.com/2008/05/28 /dining/28flavor.html.

17. "How Does Our Sense of Taste Work?," PubMed Health, last modified January 6, 2012, http://www.ncbi.nlm.nih.gov/pubmedhealth/PMH0033701.

18. Stephen P. Thornton, "Solipsism and the Problem of Other Minds," *Internet Encyclopedia of Philosophy*, accessed November 1, 2014, http://www.iep.utm .edu/solipsis.

19. Online Etymology Dictionary, s.v. "awesome," accessed April 12, 2015, http://www.etymonline.com/index.php?search=Awesome.

20. Ibid.

21. "The Official Harvey Milk Biography," Milk Foundation, accessed August 10, 2015, http://milkfoundation.org/about/harvey-milk-biography/.

22. Ibid.

23. Ibid.

24. Robert Nozick, *Anarchy, State, and Utopia* (New York: Basic Books, 1974), 42–43.

25. Peter Rubin, "The Inside Story of Oculus Rift and How Virtual Reality Became Reality," *Wired*, May 20, 2014, http://www.wired.com/2014/05 /oculus-rift-4/.

26. Adi Robertson and Michael Zelenko, "Voices from a Virtual Past: An Oral History of a Technology Whose Time Has Come Again," *Verge*, August 25, 2014, http://www.theverge.com/a/virtual-reality/oral_history.

27. Jemima Kiss, "Oculus: Facebook Buys Virtual Reality Gaming Firm for $2bn," *The Guardian*, March 25, 2014, http://www.theguardian.com /technology/2014/mar/25/facebook-buys-virtual-reality-gaming-firm-oculus.

28. Bertrand Russell, *The Analysis of Mind* (London: George Allen & Unwin, 1968), 159.

29. "The Next Black: A Film about the Future of Clothing," YouTube video, 46:55, posted by AEG, May 21, 2014, http://youtu.be/XCsGLWrfE4Y.

30. Blaine Brownwell, *Transmaterials: A Catalog of Materials That Redefine Our Physical Environment* (New York: Architectural Press, 2008), 167.

31. Ibid., 166.

32. John Haugeland, "Semantic Engines: An Introduction to Mind Design," in *Mind and Cognition: An Anthology*, 3rd ed., eds. William G. Lycan and Jesse J. Prinz (Malden, MA: Wiley-Blackwell Publishing, 2008), 195–212.

33. Brian P. McLaughlin, "Computationalism, Connectionism, and the Philosophy of Mind," in *The Blackwell Guide to the Philosophy of Computing and Information*, ed. Luciano Floridi (Malden, MA: Wiley-Blackwell Publishing, 2004), 135–151.

34. David Cole, "The Chinese Room Argument," *The Stanford Encyclopedia of Philosophy*, Spring 2014 ed., last modified April 9, 2014, http://plato.stanford .edu/archives/sum2014/entries/chinese-room.

35. Tejvan Pettinger, "Billie Holiday Biography," Biography Online, May 28, 2010, http://www.biographyonline.net/music/billie-holiday.html.

Nature

1. Scott A. Stockwell, "Scorpion Facts," Walter Reed Biosystematics Unit, accessed September 1, 2014, http://www.wrbu.org/scorpions/sc_sting.html.

2. Michele Berger, "The Most Painful Insect Stings," The Weather Channel, July 10, 2014, http://www.weather.com/news/science/most-painful-insect -stings-20130717?pageno=11.

3. "Box Jellyfish," *National Geographic*, accessed September 1, 2014, http:// animals.nationalgeographic.com/animals/invertebrates/box-jellyfish.

4. Berger, "The Most Painful Insect Stings."

5. Erica Roth, "Wasp Sting," *Healthline.com*, August 22, 2012, http://www .healthline.com/health/wasp-sting#Overview1.

6. Kathleen O'Dwyer, "The Challenge of Eternal Recurrence," *Philosophy Now*, November 1, 2014, https://philosophynow.org/issues/93/The _Challenge_of_Eternal_Recurrence.

7. Friedrich Nietzsche, *The Gay Science*, trans. Walter Kaufmann (New York: Random House, 1974), Section 341, 273.

8. Joyce Kilmer, "Trees," Poetry Foundation, accessed April 12, 2015, http:// www.poetryfoundation.org/poetrymagazine/poem/1947.

9. "Joyce Kilmer," Poetry Foundation, accessed April 12, 2015, http://www .poetryfoundation.org/bio/joyce-kilmer.

10. "Joyce Kilmer Memorial Forest," United States Department of Agriculture, Forest Service, accessed April 12, 2015, http://www.fs.usda.gov/recarea/nfsnc/null/recarea/?recid=48920&actid=70.

11. Crash Course Biology #8, "Photosynthesis," YouTube video, 13:14, posted by CrashCourse, March 19, 2012, https://www.youtube.com/watch?v=sQK3Y r4 Sc_k.

12. "The Elephants of Africa: Tale of the Trunk," *Nature*, November 16, 1997, http://www.pbs.org/wnet/nature/elephants/trunk.html.

13. Ibid.

14. Holly Williams, "How Synaesthesia Inspires Artists," *BBC.com*, October 21, 2014, http://www.bbc.com/culture/story/20140904-i-see-songs-in-colour.

15. Ibid.

16. Neil Harbisson, "I Listen to Color," TEDGlobal 2012 video, 9:35, filmed June 2012, http://www.ted.com/talks/neil_harbisson_i_listen_to_color.

17. "Marine Life You Can See Through," *New York Times*, accessed September 1, 2014, http://www.nytimes.com/slideshow/2014/08/19/science/seethrough-fish .html.

18. Ruth Williams, "Next Generation: See-Through Mice," *The Scientist*, July 31, 2014, http://www.the-scientist.com/?articles.view/articleNo/40636 /title/Next-Generation--See-through-Mice.

19. Jon Dorbolo, "Plato: Ethics—The Ring of Gyges," Oregon State, 2002, http://oregonstate.edu/instruct/phl201/modules/Philosophers/Plato/plato _dialogue_the_ring_of_gyges.html.

20. Fox Meyer, "How Octopuses and Squids Change Color," Ocean Portal, accessed September 1, 2014, http://ocean.si.edu/ocean-news/how-octopuses -and-squids-change-color.

21. Mitchell Joachim, "Don't Build Your Home, Grow It!," TED2010 video, 2:56, filmed February 2010, http://www.ted.com/talks/mitchell_joachim _don_t_build_your_home_grow_it.

22. Tuan C. Nguyen, "Scientists Turn Algae into Crude Oil in Less than an Hour," Smithsonian.com, December 31, 2013, http://www.smithsonianmag .com/innovation/scientists-turn-algae-into-crude-oil-in-less-than-an-hour -180948282.

23. Marcus Wohlsen, *Biopunk: DIY Scientists Hack the Software of Life* (New York: Penguin Group, 2011).

24. David Salisbury, "Ants Have an Exceptionally High-Def Sense of Smell," *Research News at Vanderbilt*, September 10, 2012, http://news.vanderbilt.edu /2012/09/ants-have-an-exceptionally-high-def-sense-of-smell.

25. "Planet Ant—Life Inside the Colony," BBC video, published on March 13, 2013, https://www.youtube.com/watch?v=8n0SkIGARuo.

26. Joke taken from "Water," *Look Around You*, directed by Tim Kirkby (London: BBC, 2010), DVD.

27. Emily Singer, "The Remarkable Self-Organization of Ants," *Quanta Magazine*, April 9, 2014, http://www.simonsfoundation.org/quanta/20140409 -the-remarkable-self-organization-of-ants.

28. Khalil A. Cassimally, "Why Should We Eat Insects? It's the Future of Food," *Labcoat Life* (blog), June 6, 2013, http://www.nature.com/scitable /blog/labcoat-life/why_should_we_eat_insects.

29. Daniella Martin, "Your Post-Workout Protein Shake Should Be Loaded with Insects," *Slate*, April 28, 2014, http://www.slate.com/articles/health _and_science/science/2014/04/the_benefits_of_eating_bugs_they_re_a _sustainable_efficient_and_tasty_source.html.

30. "Grub's Up," *Economist.com*, May 14, 2013, http://www.economist.com /blogs/graphicdetail/2013/05/daily-chart-11.

31. "Defect Levels Handbook," US Food and Drug Administration, accessed September 1, 2014, http://www.fda.gov/food/guidanceregulation/guidance documentsregulatoryinformation/sanitationtransportation/ucm056174.htm.

32. "Do Snakes Really Smell with Their Tongues?," AnimalSmart.org, accessed September 1, 2014, http://animalsmart.org/kids-zone/jr-animal -scientist-e-news/do-snakes-really-smell-with-their-tongues-.

33. "Arthropods: Butterfly," San Diego Zoo Animals, accessed September 1, 2014, http://animals.sandiegozoo.org/animals/butterfly.

34. "Wedding," Historical-costumes.eu, accessed September 1, 2014, http:// www.historical-costumes.eu/en/10_wedding_dresses.html.

35. "Nick Bostrom: The Simulation Argument," YouTube video, 23:27, Future of Humanity Institute, February 21, 2013, posted by Adam Ford, https:// youtu.be/nnl6nY8YKHs.

36. Jane J. Lee, "Intimate Portraits of Bees," *National Geographic*, accessed April 10, 2015, http://www.nationalgeographic.com/features/140114-bee -native-macro-photography-insects-science.

37. "Mosquito," *National Geographic*, accessed September 1, 2014, http://animals.nationalgeographic.com/animals/bugs/mosquito.

38. Janet Fang, "Ecology: A World without Mosquitoes," *Nature*, July 21, 2010, http://www.nature.com/news/2010/100721/full/466432a.html.

39. Charles Q. Choi, "How Earth's Next Supercontinent Will Form," *LiveScience*, February 9, 2015, http://www.livescience.com/18387-future-earth-supercontinent-amasia.html.

40. Thierry Bardini, "Hypertext," in *The Blackwell Guide to the Philosophy of Computing and Information*, ed. Luciano Floridi (Malden, MA: Wiley-Blackwell Publishing, 2004), 248–260.

41. Robert Nemiroff and Jerry Bonnell, "Astronomy Picture of the Day," NASA, November 4, 2007, http://apod.nasa.gov/apod/ap071104.html.

42. "About," SpaceX, accessed April 19, 2015, http://www.spacex.com/about.

43. "Elon Musk: The Case for Mars," YouTube video, 1:02, posted by SpaceX, July 9, 2013, https://youtu.be/Ndpxuf-uJHE.

44. "The Tower: Facts and Figures," Burj Khalifa, accessed January 10, 2014, http://www.burjkhalifa.ae/en/the-tower/factsfigures.aspx.

45. "Geoengineering to Combat Global Warming," United Nations Environment Programme, May 2011, http://na.unep.net/geas/getuneppage witharticleidscript.php?article_id=52.

46. Ibid.

47. "Wangari Maathai," The Green Belt Movement, accessed August 10, 2015, http://www.greenbeltmovement.org/wangari-maathai/biography.

48. "Who We Are," The Green Belt Movement, accessed August 10, 2015, http://www.greenbeltmovement.org/who-we-are.

49. "Wangari Maathai," http://www.greenbeltmovement.org/wangari-maathai/biography.

Curious Resources

Now that you know curiosity can take you anywhere, you might need some places to go. We've compiled resources for you to check out. Some of these resources are for adults, others for kids. Some of these resources are videos, some are articles, some are just interesting places on the internet. We put them all in because with a healthy dose of curiosity, you can learn anything. Remember, if you ever need to look something up, Wikipedia is an excellent place to start your knowledge quest. Speaking of which . . .

Your Curiosity

We're listing many resources here, but the most important—*beyond anything else*—is your own curiosity. Even though you live with yourself all day long, there are still new things to find and learn. Maybe a food you didn't like before now tastes great. Maybe you never realized you could achieve something your heroes do. The best way to explore yourself is to continue to try new things, learn from mistakes, and always ask questions. Your curiosity will lead you to places you've never imagined. Curiosity will disobey rules other people set up for you. It will unlock your world.

Your Local Library

Libraries not only have great books, but they also have magazines, newspapers, videos, and some even have makerspaces (community workshops with tools anyone can use). Also, they have librarians who are expert information detectives.

Books and Movies

If you ask scientists who or what inspired them, many of them will talk about science-fiction books and movies. Read new books and watch new movies. You might just be inspired to become something you never expected. Some of our favorite books are *Einstein's Dreams, Incognito: The Secret Lives of the Brain, Mrs. Frisby and the Rats of NIHM, Every Minute on Earth* (Matt's first book), and *The Boxes.* Our favorite curiosity-charging movies are *Star Wars, 2001: A Space Odyssey, Interstellar,* and *Raiders of the Lost Ark.* And, of course, the other books we mention in this section!

You can use bookshelves too. Bookshelves, really? Yep. Here's how: a bookshelf holds together many different, though usually related, ideas. Have you ever been in a library and, after finding the book you were looking for, found another really cool book in the same area? That's one way bookshelves keep your curiosity up. One of the things we find useful is that whenever we're working on a project, we can look at our bookshelves and be reminded of ideas we might have forgotten. It even helped us write this book.

Illustrated Dictionary of Cyborg Anthropology

If you appreciated the technology questions, you might want to check out Amber Case's *An Illustrated Dictionary of Cyborg Anthropology.* It inspired some of these entries. You can read more about anomie, extended nervous systems, identity production, junk sleep, persistent architecture, and more.

Physics of the Impossible

Some of our scientific entries were inspired by *Physics of the Impossible: A Scientific Exploration into the World of Phasers, Force Fields, Teleportation, and Time Travel.* The author, Michio Kaku, explains how things we've seen in science fiction might one day become reality. Or how something might never come to fruition.

What If . . . Collected Thought Experiments in Philosophy

If you liked the philosophical thought experiments and wanted to read about more, *What If . . . Collected Thought Experiments in Philosophy* by Peg Tittle is a great book to check out. Every two pages there's a new thought experiment and something new to consider.

CitizenFour

citizenfourfilm.com

You might think our section "What if Your Phone Always Knew Where You Were?" an interesting question and want to know more about what is possible with this technology. In 2014, Laura Poitras produced a documentary called *CitizenFour* that outlines a whistleblower's experience releasing private information. (Whistleblowers are people who release information to the public, in the interest of the public good, that a company, organization, or government doesn't want released.) As explained in this recounting of a true story, Edward Snowden released information that showed that the United States government has been secretly spying on American citizens and people from all over the world. This documentary is a great insight into not only what is possible but what is (or was) happening.

Cosmos

channel.nationalgeographic.com/cosmos-a-spacetime-odyssey

In 1980, Carl Sagan, a leading astronomer, had a television show that explored the quirkiness and amazingness of the universe. It was called *Cosmos*. More recently, in 2014, Neil deGrasse Tyson released an updated version of the series with him as the guide. If you want to learn more about our universe's history, human evolution, how the world works, and other oddities of our lives, *Cosmos* is the place to start.

Podcasts

Podcasts are like radio shows on the internet. Just about every subject has a podcast. If you have some free time, podcasts are great ways to keep up to date on the things you care about. Some podcasts you might enjoy are: *99% Invisible*, *This American Life*, *Song Exploder*, and *Planet Money*. Each one sheds light on things we don't always think about and does it in a way that is enjoyable and understandable.

Wikipedia.org

Encyclopedias used to be a huge collection of books with short descriptions on everything. Both of us remember when we had to look up information in a paper encyclopedia. Since 2001, the people of the internet have been contributing to a collectively built encyclopedia: Wikipedia. It has information on just about everything and is an excellent place to get started learning about something.

Like any body of work, it can sometimes have errors or biases (your teachers might remind you of this). But, when errors or biases come up, users are able to mark them so other users are aware, working together to create an always current and accurate resource. Wikipedia is where many people start a quest to learn more about something. Be sure to follow citations and never rely on only one source when you're learning about something.

DIY.org

If you liked our activities, check out DIY.org. These grouped activities can help you continue to learn about new things while also getting your hands dirty.

Business Model Generation

businessmodelgeneration.com
Have an idea for a business or nonprofit, product or service? Business Model Generation has a tool called the Business Model Canvas. It's helped both of us craft and refine our ideas. It'll probably help you too.

Crash Course, Khan Academy, Coursera

youtube.com/user/crashcourse
khanacademy.org
coursera.org
Crash Course is an online web series that gives really brief, really entertaining lessons in subjects ranging from chemistry to history to biology to psychology to literature. If you need a short video introduction to a subject, this is a great place to start.

Khan Academy and Coursera are two more places to investigate if you want to learn about something. Khan Academy is a little more math focused, and Coursera is for late high school and college students (but that doesn't mean you can't give it a shot!).

Cellular Surgeons: The New Era of Nanomedicine

youtu.be/FzFY5ms3AUc

If you're curious about nanotechnology in general or learning more about nanomedicine, you should watch this talk. Three researchers chat back and forth with a moderator about what nanotechnology is, how it works, and where their research is going.

littleBits

littlebits.cc

If you liked any of the questions that had to do with electronics, littleBits is a great way to start learning about circuits and prototyping. Each "bit" easily snaps to other bits, allowing you to build contraptions that actually do something.

Kerbal Space Program

kerbalspaceprogram.com

This video game helps keep up your adventuring spirit. We had a few questions on space, rockets, planets, the sun, more space stuff, and adventure. Here, you'll build rockets and send them into space. The destination and goal are yours to choose. Do you want to explore all the planets? Do you want to set up colonies on new planets? Do you want to create a space station? Do you want to drive rovers across alien landscapes?

Story of Stuff

storyofstuff.org/movies/story-of-stuff

Ever wonder where all this stuff around you came from? Who made it? How did it get to you? What's going to happen to it when you're done with it? This short video explains the lifecycle of the products around us with links to find out more.